MW01598763

Kurt Tucholsky

Berlin! Berlin!
Dispatches from the Weimar Republic

Berlin! Berlin!

Dispatches from the Weimar Republic

Kurt Tucholsky

Translated by Cindy Opitz

New York, 2013

Berlinica

Berlin! Berlin! Dispatches from the Weimar Republic
By Kurt Tucholsky
Translator: Cindy Opitz
Editor: Eva C. Schweitzer
Copy editor: Daniel Zitin

© 2013 by Berlinica Publishing LLC
255 West 43rd St., Suite 1012, New York, NY, 10036; USA
ISBN Print: 978-3-96026-027-1
ISBN Ebook:
978-1-935902-33-1
978-1-935902-34-8
978-1-935902-35-5
LCCN: 2012937987

Cover photo from the musical *Cabaret* live on stage at *Bar Jeder Vernunft* in the *Tipi am Kanzleramt*, www.bar-jeder-vernunft.de
Cover Photo: Joachim Gern
Design: Abstract Berlin Oslo
Model: Cora Wüthrich as a Kit-Kat girl

Photos pp. 6, 26, 41, 55, 64, 67, 120, 156, 190, 191:
Kurt Tucholsky Archiv in Marburg, Germany
Photos pp. 12, 37, 77, 109, 136, 137, 138, 165, 186:
Eva C. Schweitzer
Photos pp. 22, 29 above, 47, 60, 113, 124, 131, 174, 185:
Landesarchiv Berlin
Photos pp. 21, 173: Sonja Thomassen
Photo p. 29: Friedhelm Greis, www.weltbuehne-lesen.de

Printed in the United States
All rights reserved under International and Pan-American Copyright Law. No part of this book may be used or reproduced in any manner whatsoever without written permission except in the case of brief quotations embodied in critical articles and reviews.

www.berlinica.com

Sure, that's what you want: A mansion in the countryside with a splendid porch, the Baltic Sea in the front, Friedrichstrasse in the backyard, a sweet girl full of temperament, and another one for the weekend ...

Kurt Tucholsky on the
secret desire of every Berliner

Kurt Tucholsky, 1890–1935

Berlinica would like to thank everybody involved in the production of this book, especially the Kurt Tucholsky Gesellschaft and the Anna Maria and Stephen Kellen Foundation.

Contents

Why Kurt Tucholsky Today? Foreword by Anne Nelson   9
Kurt Tucholsky: A Berlin Life. Introduction by Ian King   13

Part I, The Beginnings: Tucholsky and His Berlin

Berlin! Berlin!   23
Three Biographies   27
To the Berlin Woman   31
The City's Face   32
Interview with Myself   38

Part II, Before the Great War: The Gilded Age

Fairy Tale   43
Harun al-Rashid   44
Berlin Cabaret   45
Summertime in Berlin   49
The Policed   51
Berlin Is Having Fun!   52
Carnival in Berlin   53
At the Movies   54
The Monitors   56

Part III, After the Great War: The Weimar Republic

Berlin's Gambling Dens   57
We Really Should Have ...   61
Flouting Love   65
White Spots   66
Berlin Business   68
In the Provinces   71
150 Kaiserallee   75
Lion on the Loose!   79
Prussian Heaven   83
The Homeless   86
A Children's Hell in Berlin   88
Three Generations   91

Berlin Love   94
Mr. Wendriner Makes a Phone Call   96
The Family   98
Mornings at Eight   101
To Do! To Do!   103
Evenings after Six   104
Ape Cage   107
Berlin's Best   110
The Lamplighters   115
The Central Office   119
Berliner on Vacation   121
Berlin Traffic   125
Mr. Wendriner Goes to the Theater   128
Confessio   132
"Just a Minute!"   134
The Slogan   139

Part IV, Impending Doom: Leaving Berlin

Berlin! Berlin!   143
Where Do the Holes in Cheese Come From?   148
Weisse with a Shot   154
The Times Are Screaming for Satire   157
In the Hotel Lobby   167
Lottie Confesses 1 Lover   171
In Defense of Berlin   175
Brief Outline of the National Economy   178
Mr. Wendriner Lives in a Dictatorship   181
Röhm   187
Afterward   189

Berlinica Presents   192

Why Kurt Tucholsky Today?

By Anne Nelson

Why Kurt Tucholsky? And why now?

Ask most Americans for their impression of Berlin in the 1920s, and they'll come up with images from *Cabaret*. Liza Minelli's "divine decadence" suggested a blend of naughty Moulin Rouge and tawdry Las Vegas. Today this seems like a distant past. But Tucholsky, who occupied the center stage in the tumultuous political and cultural world of 1920s Berlin, still emerges as an astonishingly contemporary figure. As an angry truth-teller, he pierced the hypocrisy and corruption around him with acute honesty. Imagine a writer with the acid voice of Christopher Hitchens and the satirical whimsy of Jon Stewart, combined with the iconoclasm of Bill Maher. That's Tucholsky in a nutshell.

Like Hitchens, Tucholsky wrote a mixture of literary essays, social observations, and political commentary. His irony made the line between his "serious writing" and his "entertainments" almost invisible. The fashionable outsider watched the political "center" disappear, and, in the end, he found himself catapulted out of society altogether. His career was sandwiched between the two most deadly events of his century: the bloodbath of World War I and the scourge of Nazism. Just as the first war launched Hemingway's lifelong career as a wounded tough guy with a soft spot for guns and broads, Tucholsky discovered the reflexes of an escape artist. He was equally elusive as a writer. In today's world, a journalist isn't supposed to write plays, and a playwright isn't welcomed as a novelist. But in 1920s Berlin, Tucholsky was dealing with postwar realities that required shouting from the rooftops, and any rooftop would do.

There was much to write about: Germany's damaged children, the war wounded, abounded on the streets. Dashing young soldiers returned as crippled beggars. Berlin's "divine decadence" was built on the lives of young women whose sweethearts had been slaughtered at the front and whose dowries vanished in the hyperinflation and the Great Depression. They were driven first to pawn their possessions, then to strip in seedy clubs, and finally to drugs and prostitution.

In 1913, Tucholsky had started writing for a theater publication called *Die Schaubühne*. After World War I, German politics jumped onto the stage and German theater leapt into politics. *Die Schaubühne*, or "theater stage," changed its name to *Die Weltbühne*, or "world stage," run initially by Siegfried Jacobson and then Carl von Ossietzky. It assembled many of the most daring authors. One was playwright Walter Hasenclever, whom Tucholsky had recruited in 1920s Paris. Others were Richard Hülsenbeck, and Ernst Toller, whose antiwar play *Hoppla, wir Leben* (Hooray We're Alive!) contained the line, "There's only one thing to do: either hang oneself or change the world." One of the best-known contributors was Erich Mühsam, who published a passionate outpouring of poetry, essays, plays, and cabaret songs. These writers spanned many categories: Christians, Jews and atheists; anarchists, Communists and Socialists. What they shared was a personal experience of the war, the contempt for the political system that caused it, and the black humor to satirize it.

At the center of the debate was the concept of "cosmopolitanism." In an era of hypernationalism, the idea of being a "citizen of the cosmos" is dangerous. Just as many Americans in the heartland consider New York City as "den of iniquity," the German *Volk* were deeply suspicious of multicultural Berlin. The Nazis cherished a particular hatred for the city; Goebbels swore to conquer it, and Hitler called it a "rubble field" (years before he turned it into one).

Germany experienced massive immigration and political dislocation over the early twentieth century, which gave rise to a sharp cultural divide. The population in the countryside was largely homogeneous in its ethnic, religious and linguistic makeup, while major cities were growing increasingly diverse. This was especially true of Berlin, with its many White Russians and Jews fleeing the pogroms of Eastern Europe. In good economic times, cosmopolitanism made the city a cultural magnet. In hard times, ugly rhetoric emerged about foreigners stealing jobs and immigrants who couldn't speak the language properly. This prejudice generated institutionalized racism and anti-intellectualism, which was also directed against liberal, urban Jewish Germans. Rational discourse degenerated into threats and brawls. Socialists and pacifists were vilified for the so-called stab-in-the-back-treaty that ended the First World War. Contemporary Americans who are worried about the decline of tolerance and civility in their political culture can find further cause in this history.

The disaster began in 1930: The Versailles Treaty had forbidden Germany to rearm, but one of the *Weltbühne's* reporters found evidence that Germany was violating the agreement. In a foreshadowing of Wikileaks, Ossietzky and Tucholsky decided to publish. Ossietzky was arrested. He was convicted of treason and espionage and sentenced to eighteen months in prison. When the Nazis took power in 1933, he was sent to a concentration camp, where he died. Mühsam was sent to a succession of concentration camps before he was beaten to death by Storm Troopers in 1934.

Other *Weltbühne* authors scattered to the four winds; Paris and New York swarm with their ghosts. Walter Hasenclever escaped back to France, where, ironically, he was interned by the French as an "enemy alien." He committed suicide in the internment camp in 1940, as the Germans were invading, to avoid falling into Nazi hands. Ernst Toller made it to New York, but hung himself in the Mayflower Hotel in 1939. Richard Hülsenbeck was the lucky one. He escaped to New York and reinvented himself as a psychoanalyst named Charles Hulbeck, practicing for decades on Central Park West. Tucholsky himself had fled to Sweden, and took his life in 1935.

Kurt Tucholsky and his friends are little known outside Germany these days. It is hard to convey the tremendous energy and urgency they brought to the political and cultural life of their time. We may experience their echo as the fading notes of "Come to the cabaret." But these men staked their lives on the idea that freedom of expression is a human right, that art can overcome war, and that hypocrisy and greed can be punctured by satirical songs and well-chosen words. These values are more immediate today than ever.

Anne Nelson is an author and playwright who specializes in media and international affairs from a human rights perspective; she wrote *The Red Orchestra: The Story of the Berlin Underground and the Circle of Friends Who Resisted Hitler.* She teaches at Columbia University.

Tucholskystrasse, named after the author, at the corner of Oranienburger Strasse in Berlin-Mitte, with the New Synagogue, 2012.

Kurt Tucholsky: A Berlin Life

By Ian King

When Tucholsky started to write, his noms de plume gave him five "voices"—yet in the end, he had none. He had been one of the most famous journalists in Weimar Germany, but he died alone in Sweden, divorced, penniless, and an official enemy of the new German state. He was among the first authors whose books were burned by the Nazis in 1933. But Kurt Tucholsky—the brilliant satirist, journalist, lyricist, pacifist, and democrat, the fighter and lady's man—is not forgotten.

First and foremost, he sounded an early warning against militarism and the Nazis, who hated him and drove him out of his country. Second, he opposed the other reactionary forces in German society—the judges, top civil servants, university professors, press barons and conservative bourgeoisie—who even after the halfhearted revolution of 1918–19 had retained their influential positions and used them to sabotage Germany's first attempt at a democratic republic. Third, he fought for the "ordinary Joes," on fundamentally ethical grounds: "We fight out of love for the oppressed ... and we love in human beings the idea of humankind." All this made him, in the words of Erich Kästner, his journalistic colleague and contemporary, the "small, fat Berliner," who "wanted to stop a catastrophe with his typewriter."

Tucholsky's criticism of German society, his antimilitarism, courage, left-wing beliefs and love of life and his admonitions about fascism and right-wing ideologues are still relevant today and deserve to be rediscovered. But Tucholsky was not only a political animal; he was also a Berliner, born and bred. He had a complicated love-hate relationship with his hometown. Yet Berlin, the Prussian metropolis that grew tremendously before the turn of the nineteenth century, always challenged him. Berliners often drove him crazy, elbowing their way through the city with their loud, know-it-all, tough-kid attitudes. He satirized their ability to talk fast yet say nothing, and their inability to listen to one another, whether in person or on the telephone. Whereever ringtones are to be heard and dogs bark incessantly, Tucholsky's dislike of "noise and din" will meet a sympathetic response.

Still, he always defended Berlin against the backward conservative countryside. In his writing, he created many quintessential Berlin characters: "Herr Wendriner," the fidgety and rather conservative Jewish businessman; Lottchen, the unfaithful flapper; the loud-mouthed Berliner in show business; the heartless Prussian bureaucrat and the people who obeyed him; and the careless partygoers who spent far too much money from shady sources.

Tucholsky was born on January 9, 1890, to a Jewish family in the Berlin district of Moabit. A plaque at his birthplace at 13 Lübecker Strasse recalls his life and work, along with a Kindergarten named "Tiger, Panter, and Co.," the slightly misquoted title of a postwar anthology of his works. His father, Alex Tucholsky, worked his way up to become a director of the Berliner Handelsgesellschaft, a major bank, but he died when only fifty.

Kurt had a difficult relationship with his domineering mother, Doris, later to perish in the Theresienstadt concentration camp. He also had two younger siblings, Fritz and Ellen. Due to his father's job, young Kurt spent his first years in Stettin on the Baltic Sea and returned to Berlin with his family at the age of nine. He attended the Französisches Gymnasium (French Secondary School) and the Königliche Wilhelms Gymnasium (Royal King Wilhelm Secondary School), and later studied law in Berlin and Geneva. He traveled early on, meeting Max Brod and Franz Kafka in Prague and making an impression on both. Tucholsky never worked as an attorney because he began writing for newspapers while still a student.

His first article appeared in 1907, in *Der Ulk* (The Joke), the satirical weekly supplement to Rudolf Mosse's centrist daily, *Berliner Tageblatt*. He was only seventeen at the time. The piece was a short satire on Kaiser Wilhelm's unenlightened artistic tastes, and he continued to despise Wilhelm's vainglorious vulgarity and reckless warmongering, even after the latter's enforced abdication and flight in 1918. He also was engaged in politics early on; he wrote for the left-wing Social Democrats in 1911, Germany's oldest political party. His first book came out one year later, *Rheinsberg, ein Bilderbuch für Verliebte* (Rheinsberg, A Picturebook for Lovers), a romantic and humorous short story with drawings by his friend Kurt Szafranski. To boost sales, they opened a temporary "book bar" on Kurfürstendamm; everyone who bought a book got a free shot of liquor.

In January 1913, Tucholsky started what would turn out to be the longest relationship in his life: writing for *Die Schaubühne* (The Stage), a small theatrical paper with a circulation of about a thousand, that in 1918 was renamed *Die Weltbühne* (The World Stage) and became more political and influential (it was closed by the Nazis after the Reichstag fire). *Weltbühne* publisher and editor Siegfried Jacobsohn became his teacher and mentor. Tucholsky wrote a number of articles for most issues, in many sections of the paper, so he invented four pseudonyms: Ignaz Wrobel, Peter Panter, Theobald Tiger, and, somewhat later, Kaspar Hauser. Each of these characters had a different personality and voice, with the goal of making *Die Weltbühne* seem more diverse (in this book, the bylines are left as they were originally published). Not just Tucholsky, but quite a few other famous left-wingers from Berlin's cultural scene wrote for *Die Weltbühne*, from Alfred Polgar to Arnold Zweig and Walter Hasenclever.

In World War I, Tucholsky was drafted, like most German men of his age. He took great care not to get shot, or to shoot anyone else. He claimed that once he intentionally left his gun behind—certainly he came back in one piece, and as a committed pacifist to boot. To avoid further fighting on the Eastern front, he created and edited a military paper for the air force, *Der Flieger* (The Pilot). In the Latvian military base of Alt Autz he met his future wife, Mary Gerold, though he was to marry (and divorce) another woman first, his former friend from student days, Dr. Else Weil. His superior, Erich Danehl, managed to get him transferred to Romania as a military police officer. Danehl later became one of Tucholsky's best friends and moonlights in some of his stories as "Karlchen."

Upon his discharge from military service, Tucholsky became the editor of *Der Ulk,* and also began to work for *Die Weltbühne* again, taking a strong antimilitaristic stand. He wrote for a number of papers, initially for the *Berliner Tageblatt* and its more progressive stablemate, the *Berliner Volkszeitung*. In March 1920, weary of the coalition government's unsuccessful compromises with the old regime, he joined the left-wing Independent Social Democratic Party (USPD) and contributed satires, election pieces and even a detailed analysis of the inflated military budget to its newspapers, *Die Freiheit* and *Freie Welt*. But he needed to survive on the proceeds of his journalistic work, and so he also wrote for the government-financed newspaper *Pieron*, which was strongly anti-Polish.

In accordance with the Versailles Treaty that ended World War I, Germany had to cede parts of West Prussia, Posen, and Silesia to Poland (as well as Alsace-Lorraine to France), against which the *Pieron* fought aggressively. The assignment paid very well, but Tucholsky later came to regret his involvement, especially since his friends in the USPD initially gave him a hard time about it. He also began to write couplets for chanteuses like Claire Waldoff, the Berlin gamine who would go on to achieve considerable fame.

Today, the Roaring Twenties in Berlin are remembered for their cabarets, nightlife, and for sex, drugs, and music—from Marlene Dietrich and Lotte Lenya to the dancer Anita Berber. But for most people, the 1920s were tough times. Millions of German soldiers had been killed or crippled in World War I; hundreds of thousands of children had starved or had died of diseases during or after the war. Widows prostituted themselves in the streets of Berlin to save their families from hunger. A great deal of money changed hands on the black market, most of it semi-legally, at best.

After the Kaiser fled to the Netherlands, the Weimar Republic was proclaimed from the Reichstag balcony in 1918 by Social Democratic politician Philipp Scheidemann. But the Republic remained shaky. Right-wing militarists were fighting—and killing—disillusioned revolutionaries and republicans in the hundreds on the streets of Berlin, Munich, Hamburg, the cities of the Ruhr and elsewhere in Germany; politicians were assassinated, among them Rosa Luxemburg and Karl Liebknecht, the founders of the German Communist Party, as well as Walter Rathenau, Germany's first Jewish foreign minister, a moderate liberal rather than a left-winger.

Also, hyperinflation destroyed the German currency, put workers on the breadline and broke the back of the middle class, while the few who had access to American dollars, or owned land, factories or other property had the chance to become very rich indeed. After a brief reprieve during the second half of the 1920s, unemployment climbed into the millions. Tucholsky spent that time fighting as well—for the Republic, against militarism and the Prussian bureaucracy, and against a biased justice system that favored right-wingers and monarchists. In 1922, problems in his first marriage to Else Weil, along with Germany's increasingly disastrous political and economic state, led him into bouts of depression and an apparent suicide attempt. The following year's runaway inflation drove him to work at a bank to support himself. There he found plenty of material for the later Wendriner monologues—some of them included in this book—but journalism was his vocation.

However, in the spring of 1924 he began to write much more regularly again for *Die Weltbühne*. He went to Paris as a correspondent for that paper, as well as for the centrist *Vossische Zeitung*. He also divorced Else and married Mary Gerold. Mary went to Paris with him—but their life together turned out to be more difficult than she had expected, because Tucholsky spent a lot of time with his typewriter, fulfilling his journalistic obligations to produce essays, reviews and poems. He, however, felt at home in Paris, much like Heinrich Heine, an earlier German-Jewish writer. He wrote some pieces in which he compared Paris to Berlin and cast the latter in a rather unflattering light. But he was called back to Berlin in December 1926, after Siegfried Jacobsohn died, to become editor of *Die Weltbühne*.

He never warmed to the job, though, being more of a soloist than a conductor, and after six months relinquished his position to colleague Carl von Ossietzky. Tucholsky published a book about a vacation in the Pyrenees, the mountains between Spain and France, and the short novel *Schloss Gripsholm* (Gripsholm Castle) in 1931, set in Sweden, which in the postwar period was to become his best-selling work. He also met Lisa Matthias in the beginning of 1927 (on whom the character "Lottchen" is based). He divorced Mary in 1933 after the Nazis came to power, mainly in order to protect her.

When Paul von Hindenburg, Germany's defeated military leader in the First World War and a Prussian monarchist, was elected president in 1925, Tucholsky had already been deeply concerned. A succession of backward-looking conservative governments as well as repeated examples of judicial bias against working-class defendants confirmed his fear that the Republic had fallen into the hands of its enemies. Though the Social Democrats remained in the Prussian coalition government, he concluded that their plans to gradually establish democracy had been a failure. The Weimar state now appeared as class-ridden as the empire that preceded it. Like many independent left-wing intellectuals, he was attracted to some ideas of Marxism and by the Communist workers, who seemed to be the one remaining progressive force in his country.

He even sought to work with, though not within, the Communist ranks, publishing some forty poems and articles in the *Arbeiter Illustrierte Zeitung* (Workers' Illustrated Paper) in the late 1920s. The controversial anthology ironically entitled *Deutschland, Deutschland Über Alles,* was savagely critical of militarism, of the threat of another war, and the yawning social gap between rich and poor; the book, featuring photomontages by John Heartfield, was realeased by a Communist publishing house.

Yet paradoxically it also contained a different tone: "After 225 pages of saying 'No,' out of pity, love, hatred, and passion we finally, just once, want to say 'yes' to Germany, the land in which we were born and whose language we speak," he wrote on the last page. "Because the Nationalists, who are really bourgeois militarists, don't own this country. We are here as well, and part of it." Probably Tucholsky already sensed that his attempt to work alongside the Communists would founder on the party's dogmatism and unthinking obedience to the Moscow line. The search for common ground ended in failure.

Tucholsky understood early on the danger the Nazis presented; in 1930, he went to Sweden. He spent most of these years traveling. Yet he still warned repeatedly against the fascist danger, exposed the party's industrialist paymasters and its petit-bourgeois mass membership and scornfully satirized its spokesman in Berlin, Joseph Goebbels. Colleagues who remained in Germany suffered much more. Carl von Ossietzky, his editor, had to stand trial for treason: *Die Weltbühne* had disclosed that the German army was secretly rearming—expressly forbidden by the Versailles Treaty. In November, 1931, Ossietzky was sentenced to eighteen months in jail.

Tucholsky did not go to Berlin to come to Ossietzky's defense, fearing he would end up in jail too—having been indicted for his famous line "Soldiers are murderers," he wrote in *Die Weltbühne* three months prior. But for many years to come, he felt like a coward for staying in Sweden. "I failed," he wrote to his estranged wife Mary Gerold, "I failed due to laziness, cowardice, loathing, and contempt ... even though I could not have helped him, even though we both would have been sentenced, I know all that, but I still feel guilty."

After 1932, Tucholsky fell silent. He suffered from a serious sinus problem that caused constant headaches and made it difficult for him to sleep or even breathe. He and Lisa Matthias had split up, and his depression returned. In letters to one of his last girlfriends, the Swiss doctor Hedwig Müller whom he called "Nuuna," he described himself as a "discontinued German," and a "discontinued poet." Finally, he wrote to colleague Walter Hasenclever, "From now on, I'll just shut up. You can't whistle against the ocean."

After Tucholsky's (and Ossietzky's) books were burned by the Nazis on Berlin's Opernplatz in 1933, his German citizenship was revoked and his bank accounts were confiscated by the regime. He recognized that Hitler would not fall from power any time soon. And he knew that war was looming. Ossietzky had been tortured in a concentration camp, and Tucholsky tried to help him. He attempted to convince the Nobel Peace Prize Committee to give the 1935 prize to Ossietzky. But the Norwegians hesitated, though they changed their minds and gave him the award a year later (Ossietzky, however, died of tuberculosis in 1938). Tucholsky also attacked German Jews for neither resisting the Nazis nor leaving Germany. "I have seen 'our people' face to face, and I understood," he wrote to Arnold Zweig, who had emigrated to Palestine. "I'm done with Germany; I have nothing to do with it anymore—let it die; let Russia conquer it."

In his last months, Tucholsky required continual medical care. He came to see Mary Gerold as the one true love of his life. "I had a gold nugget in my hands and threw it away for pennies," he wrote. On December 21, 1935, his friends found him in a coma. It was assumed that he had committed suicide, though it has also been suggested that it might have been an accidental overdose. He was buried in the Swedish town of Mariefred, near Gripsholm Castle.

On January 10, 1936, three weeks after his death, *The New York Times* published his obituary. "More than any other person, he foresaw what was coming there, and that was one of the reasons why after the Nazi revolution he virtually never wrote anything on the subject," the *Times* wrote. The obituary added: "'I wrote about it all years ago,' he said to friends. 'There's nothing left for me to add.' What his readers had enjoyed as the capricious fantasies of a clever satirist has now been enacted in bitter reality—even to a satirical forecast of his own mode of death."

Kurt Tucholsky, however, lives on in the words he left behind. Since 1945, as a result initially of devoted efforts by his widow, his works have been read by millions more than during his lifetime, and translated into fourteen languages, from Portuguese to Japanese. This is the first collection of his Berlin stories in English.

His writings still have lessons for us today: that a man who might have preferred to write idylls, humorous pieces and unpolitical verse instead devoted his life to fighting against injustice and arguing passionately against the addiction to military uniforms which afflicted too many of his compatriots.

Like Cassandra, Tucholsky warned his people to turn back from their chosen path to perdition, and as with the Trojan priestess, his people ignored the advice. Can we today avoid similar mistakes?

Ian King is the chair of the *Kurt Tucholsky Gesellschaft* in Germany since 2009, and a former university professor of German in Sheffield and London, UK, who now works as a translator. He was awarded a doctorate in 1977 by his home university, Glasgow in Scotland, for his thesis on Kurt Tucholsky's political development. He was also co-editor of Volume 3 of Tucholsky's Complete Works and has lectured on the subject in the UK, Germany, Israel and Norway.

Kurt Tucholsky in Paris in 1928, after he left Berlin to become a foreign correspondent for Die Weltbühne.

Potsdamer Platz, the heart of Berlin between East and West, and in the 1920s the place with arguably the most traffic in Europe.

Part I
The Beginnings:
Tucholsky and His Berlin

Berlin! Berlin!

Ignaz Wrobel, Berliner Tageblatt, July 21, 1919

Quanquam ridentem dicere verum
Quid vetat? *

There's no sky above this city. Whether the sun shines at all is questionable; it seems like you only ever see the sun when you're crossing the main boulevard and it's shining right in your eyes. People complain about the weather, but there really isn't any weather in Berlin.

A Berliner doesn't have time. A Berliner is usually from Posen or Breslau, and he doesn't have time. He always has plans, and he makes phone calls and appointments, and he rushes to his appointments—usually running late—and he has such an awful lot to do.

People don't work in this city—they slave away. (Even entertainment is work here; they spit in their hands at the start and expect to get something in return.) A Berliner isn't really diligent, just constantly agitated. He has completely forgotten, unfortunately, why we're here on this earth. Even in heaven—assuming a Berliner could make it to heaven—he would "have things to do" at four.

Sometimes you see Berlin women sitting on the balconies that are stuck to the stone boxes they call their homes. The Berlin women sit there, taking breaks. They might be between two phone conversa-

---

* "What forbids telling the truth while laughing?" Horace, *Satires* I.1.

tions, or waiting for appointments, or they may have arrived early—which rarely happens—so they sit there and wait. Then suddenly they spring, like arrows launched from bowstrings, to the telephone or to their next appointments.

This city is forever hauling its cart around the same track, brow furrowed—*sit venia verbo!* It doesn't notice it's going in circles and getting nowhere.

A Berliner can't have a normal conversation. Sometimes you see two people talking, but they're not having a conversation, they're just reciting their own monologues to each other. Berliners can't listen either. They just wait anxiously until the other person stops talking and then jump right in. That's how Berliners converse.

A Berlin woman is practical and clear. Even in love. She doesn't have any secrets. She's a good, sweet girl, a type much celebrated by gallant town poets.

A Berliner doesn't get much out of life unless he's earning money. He doesn't cultivate social skills, because he can't be bothered; he gets together with friends, gossips a little, and gets sleepy at ten o'clock.

A Berliner is a slave to the machine—passenger, theatergoer, restaurant patron, and employee. Not quite human. The machine picks and pulls at his nerve endings, and a Berliner submits without reservation. He does everything the city requires—except maybe live.

A Berliner plows through each day, and when it's done, it was all labor and sorrow, nothing more. A Berliner can live in this city for seventy years without the slightest benefit to his immortal soul.

Berlin was once a well-functioning machine. A finely crafted doll that could move its arms and legs when someone stuck a dime in it. Today, the doll barely moves; no matter how many dimes people throw in, the machine has rusted and grown sluggish.

Because there really are a lot of strikes in Berlin. Why? No one really knows. Some people are against it, and some people are for it. Why? No one really knows.

Berliners treat each other like hostile strangers. If they haven't been introduced somewhere, they snarl at each other in the streets and on the trolleys, because they don't have much in common. They don't

---

* Latin for "excuse that expression."

want to know anything about anyone else, and they live entirely for themselves.

Berlin combines the disadvantages of an American metropolis with those of small-town Germany. Its advantages are listed in Baedeker's guidebooks.

During summer vacation each year, a Berliner sees that people actually live in the real world. He tries it for four weeks—unsuccessfully, because he hasn't learned how to live and doesn't truly know what it means—and when he arrives back at the Anhalter train station, he winks at the trolley line and is glad to be back in Berlin. Life is forgotten again.

The days rattle by, and the daily grind winds on; if we toil like this for a hundred years, we in Berlin, what then for us? Will we have accomplished anything? Achieved anything? Something for our lives, for our real-life actual, inner lives? Will we have grown, opened ourselves up, blossomed? Will we have lived?

Berlin! Berlin!

When the editor had read up to this point, he wrinkled his brow, smiled a friendly smile, and said benevolently to the young man standing before him, "Well, now, it's really not as bad as all that! You're forgetting that Berlin also has its merits and accomplishments! Take it easy, young man! You're still young!"

And because the young man was a rather polite young man, generally loved and respected for his modest behavior, possessing somewhat peculiar dance-class manners, which he passed off as etiquette among close friends, he took off his hat (which he'd kept on in the room), gazed, deeply moved, at the ceiling, and cried with pious conviction, "God bless this city!"

Left: *Kurt Tucholsky as a one-year-old baby in 1891.*

Below: *Tucholsky (at right), with his younger siblings Ellen (left) and Fritz (middle), in 1904. He was a student at the French Grammar School in Berlin at the time.*

Three Biographies

Peter Panter, Die Weltbühne, *June 1, 1926*

"You're the unborn Peter Panter?" asked the Good Lord, stroking his white beard, which was flecked with gray here and there. I was a bright blob floating in my test tube; I hopped up and down in affirmation. "You have three possibilities," the Heavenly Father said, squashing a bedbug in infinite benevolence as it scurried across his wrist. "Three possibilities. Please consider each one and tell me which you choose. We're particularly interested in not favoring either party in the current dispute between Determinists and Indeterminists. You figure out up here what you'd like to be someday; down there you won't be able to do anything about it. If you please ..." The Old Man held a large box lid up to the tube, on which I read:

I

"Peter Panter (1st Draft). Born on April 15, 1889, son of poor but well sanitized parents, in Stettin on Lasztownia Island. Father: Given to quarterly episodes of binge drinking, with five quarters each year. Mother: Subscribes to the *Berliner Lokal-Anzeiger*. Studies veterinary medicine in Hannover and becomes a municipally licensed exterminator in Halle in 1912. Two wives: Annemarie Prellwitz, classy, in flannel, with her hair in buns (1919–1924); Ottilie Mann, meticulous, proper, tremendously fertile, in balloon cloth (1925–1937). Four sons; then acquires a German Persian rug. 1931: Cleans Hermann Bahr's beard; Bahr survives, and P. converts to Catholicism. Summoned to Vienna in June, 1948, to eradicate the bedbugs accumulating at the *Neues Wiener Journal's* cultural desk. When the operation naturally fails, exterminator P. becomes depressed. In this state of mind, attends a Keyserling lecture on April 20, 1954. Dies: April 21. Panter departs from life, with the consolation of the Catholic Church, immediately after voraciously devouring a bowl of matzo balls. Burial weather: partly cloudy with a light southeasterly wind.

Headstone (designed by Paul Westheim): 100.30 marks; marble price: 100 marks. Forever cherished in our thoughts: eight months."

"Well?" asked the Almighty God.

"Hmm …" I said. And read on:

II

"Peter Panter (2nd Draft). Born May 8, 1891, eldest son of senior civil servant Panter and his wife Gertrud, née Hauser. The premature child is so hard of hearing in his left ear as a young boy that he already seems destined for a career in justice. Joins the fraternity corps, in which a certain Niedner is an alum—" God Almighty made the sign of the swastika. I continued to read: "—and soon adopts the properly boorish behavior expected in such circles. 1918: War assessor, just in time for the Kaiser's birthday. Swears eternal loyalty to him. 1919: Junior assistant to the state commissioner of public policy; State Commissioner Weismann, in accordance with traditional Prussian frugality, does not sit in an armchair but remains on a wooden bench day and night. District Court Councilor P. achieves great things for the Republic and its president. Swears him eternal loyalty. Participates in the Kapp Putsch in 1920, advises Kapp in judicial matters and swears eternal loyalty to him. Panter's frequent swearing calls attention to the talented jurist, and he is transferred to the post of chief legal counsel to the Reichswehr. Meanwhile, Rathenau is murdered, and the Republic imposes a constitutional court on itself, in which decisions are made without due process. Transfers there as judge; sprains his arm signing jail sentences for Communists in 1924. No funeral is held, as a German judge is irremovable and can still fulfill the duties of his office even after death."

"How could anyone sink so low?" the Good Lord asked. I, meanwhile, had crept to the bottom of the test tube. I wagged my little tail, and God Almighty correctly guessed "No," made the sign of the Star of David, and held up number …

III

"Peter Panter (3rd Draft). Born January 9, 1890, in Berlin, with gigantic nostrils. His Aunt Berta looked in his cradle and said so immediately. Succeeds with minimal effort in becoming a decent

Above: *Siegfried Jacobsohn, whom Tucholsky called S.J., a lifelong mentor, friend and his first editor at* Die Schaubühne *(Theater Stage) and* Die Weltbühne *(World Stage), the paper Tucholsky worked for most of his adult life. When Jacobsohn died in 1926 at age 45, Carl von Ossietzky replaced him as the editor.*

man, then falls into the clutches of publisher S.J., who employs him in a variety of tasks; at the beginning of their acquaintance, P. writes articles and poems, and after just fifteen years, he's allowed to put stamps on letters on his own and execute other important clerical tasks. January 19, 1913: Contracts with the publisher for a monthly honorarium. December 8, 1936: Notice of first installment. Assumes the pseudonyms Max Jungnickel, Mark Twain, Waldemar Bonsels, and Fritz von Unruh. Can never convince anyone that there's more than one author behind these names. Painted in oil by Professor Liebermann; gives him a Paul Klee original in return, though Liebermann doesn't eat it up. S.J. bequeaths Panter his son; P. knocks large holes in the expensive heirloom's head in the very first week and doesn't handle him very gently in other ways either. Dies on July 4, 1976, while attempting to tear the publisher back out of his grave."

"Well?" the Good Lord asked.

"Hmm," I said again, "Can't we combine all three biographies? Maybe I could be the son of a senior civil servant, and exterminator at the *Weltbühne* ..."

"Hurry up!" Father God said sternly, "I don't have much time. I'm presiding over three field services at ten o'clock: Poles versus the Germans, Germans versus the Poles, and the Italians versus everyone else. I must go be with my peoples. So choose."

And so I chose.*

---

* Here, T. mocks the authoritarian militaristic tradition of Germany under the Kaiser (who fled in 1919, after World War I). "1st Draft" depicts a son raised in an über-assimilated petit-bourgeois Jewish household; T. mentions a number of conservative newspapers, artists, and authors he doesn't like, especially Hermann Alexander Graf Keyserling. "2nd Draft" depicts a stereotypical right-winger and refers to several Weimar political figures, namely Alexander Niedner, a judge who sentenced three Communists to death, Robert Weismann, a frugal politician who later fled the Nazis, and Walter Rathenau, the first Jewish Foreign Minister, murdered in 1922 by right-wingers. The Kapp Putsch was a failed military coup against the Weimar Republic in 1920. "3rd Draft" is a satirical coloration of T.'s actual life (the "pseudonyms" are names of real authors); Max Liebermann and Paul Klee are painters (*Klee* is also the German word for "clover," hence the reference to eating it). S.J. is Siegfried Jacobsohn, the editor of the *Weltbühne*.

To the Berlin Woman

Theobald Tiger, Die Weltbühne, March 23, 1922

Girl, no Casanova
would ever impress you.
Could some daft lover's
fantasy really prove true?
If love-vanquished Romeo
were to sing with nostrils flared,
you would softly whisper,
"Are you whacked in the head?"
When it's romance
you're wanting,
a movie you'll take in. . .
You're Mother's bestest darling,
you, woman of Berlin!

Spree-River Venus, how busy
your love, so punctual you!
Flirting until twelve-thirty,
kissing till the wee hour of two.
Dispatching all things like a pro,
your oath of love well met,
all tidy, clean, and factual:
You're a living file cabinet!
No matter how hard he presses
you to him, you won't give in.
Indeed, you're Mother's bestest,
you, woman of Berlin!

Weekdays you
employ, we know,
gladly ruler and needle.
But on Sundays the
stars do glow,
so Prussianly sentimental.
Thinking of that
moleskin stole,
your boyfriend bought for you?
Filmstar Pola's*
shining example,
draped like she, you
shimmy, too.
As you simply age, the rest
will whither with the years.
No need for swanky gestures!
For you are darling
Mother's best,
sweet woman of Berlin!

---

* Pola Negri, a Polish-born dancer
and silent film star in Berlin, famous
for femme fatale roles. In 1922 she
became the first continental European star to move to Hollywood.

The City's Face

Ignaz Wrobel, Freiheit, November 16, 1920

"… the tragic fate—of growing from a Wendish fishing community into a powerful metropolis and imperial capital—that damns Berlin: ever becoming and never to be."
—Karl Scheffler, Berlin

We don't say "berlinerisch"; we say "berlinisch," and that's what we are.[*]

From a weak little royal seat, this, our city, was suddenly elevated, after the pseudo-victory of the war of 1870–71, by the industrial expansion of Germany's gilded age. Bright façades and tarted-up merchants' wives, whose new wealth didn't quite agree with them, made for a strange mix with the old Prussian heritage of the Kaiser and his officers and officials. While the wealth did not exactly become Prussian, the Prussians did become gilded in gold, to the detriment of the Potsdam style that had previously ruled in the city. Wilhelm, that national disaster, finished the city. Those with a knack for geological prospecting will know where to look for these three layers throughout Berlin, with their three-fold vestiges: good old Berlin, Berlin of the gilded age, and the Wilhelminian/wartime Berlin. Because what the national press—which should never page through its wartime volumes, crawling as they are with false prophecies, erroneous assumptions, and ruinous advice—what the national press attributes to the revolution in Berlin today can be traced back to August 1, 1914.

The decline of paradise for the middle class and the birth of a new city—both began back then, when the alleys echoed with the clamor of pathetic lunatics setting out to conquer the world and

---

[*]   *Berlinerisch* is a term out-of-towners and newcomers use; *Berlinisch* is how born-and-bred Berliners refer to themselves.

returning home again with nothing more than a bit of Brussels lace, a few stolen pigs, and syphilis. It was then, on August 1, that this new Berlin arose. But which ... ?

First of all, a different one. That's the main tune everyone's singing today. "Father of mine! How you've changed!" For it's no longer the same city, no longer the one through which the Kaiser paraded the exhausted, sweaty proletarian uniforms, through the enthusiastic and appropriately cordoned-off streets. It's still called Berlin. But that's no longer what it is.

After a couple of wild months around New Year's 1918—the only time anything resembling fresh air ever blew over Prussia, despite horrible mistakes, civil wars, all hell breaking loose, riots, and shootouts: fresh air ("Gee, thanks!" says the frugal citizen)—after that, Berlin developed quickly and logically, sliding ever further to the east.

This colonial city had to endure a deluge of Eastern Jews, Poles, and Russians—had to take in the first swarm of elements trying their luck in the cultured West. These Easterners don't, as that Teutonic nationalist Wulle suspects, spread Bolshevism—they are mostly its enemy. But they do change Berlin.

Helfferich's economics and Ludendorff's sloppiness sucked the city dry.* Gone was the salvation of the middle class; gone were Kempinski and cheap entertainment—and how typically berlinisch, that a young mail clerk out on the town with twenty marks in his pocket before the war got by downright lavishly, from his point of view. That didn't happen in any other city—in other places there was above and below and nothing in between. The middle class once dominated in Berlin, which never had hugely rich people, because they either left the city or never bothered to come in the first place.

That was then. The middle class is eroding, slowly but surely—

---

* T. is referring to German right-wingers he despises. Reinhold Wulle was an anti-Semitic activist with the *Deutschvölkische Freiheitspartei* (the German People's Freedom Party). Karl Theodor Helfferich was a right-wing opposition leader in the Reichstag and Treasury Secretary during WWI. Erich Ludendorff was a WWI general who blamed Social Democrats and Jews for Germany's war defeat. Berthold Kempinski opened a four-story restaurant in Berlin in 1889 bearing his name, which became wildly popular; but was "aryanized" by the Nazis.

even today, the carefully preserved posture of the bourgeoisie is often just a thin veneer, and they're drifting upward or downward: upward—the ones who profit from wars and revolutions; downward—the proletarianized masses. People coming here from abroad show us what we've become. Someone once told me, "Everyone's face here looks downright mean!" That's probably true. The daily grind etches them deeply—fighting with housing departments, landlords, rationing systems, and bureaucrats for real-life necessities takes its toll. Because this is Rule No.1 in Berlin: Nothing's allowed, and everything's done under the table.

No one is honest. No one can be, because the Prussians, having misunderstood the responsibilities of government, issue regulations that cannot possibly be complied with. So people circumvent them.

Their stories vary. The prostitute at Schlesische Station, the bookie, the shopkeeper, the tenant, the housewife—no one gets by without graft. The government is strangling them with red tape. And the vitality of these nameless ones is formidable, their tenacity unprecedented, in refusing to let anything bring them down. Foolhardiness? Dear God, who can be foolish here? It's simply the brutish joy at still being here—not lying in Flanders or Turkey—and not, under any circumstances whatsoever, letting life become any worse than the salaried bureaucrats make it.

The thing that the city completely took over from peacetime was its pace. Not an American pace (too impractical for that)—but one that's thoroughly berlinisch, and it's contagious. (This pace is also clearly evident in the art of enjoying oneself here, where amusement is a chore.) That's one thing the new Berlin took over from the old one. But the look and sound are completely different.

First of all, the money came into different hands—fatter, fleshier, flabbier hands. The honest faces in the nightclubs usually belong to the waiters, and those gracing the theater boxes pretty much ruin the whole facade. Who else can … ?

Hey, they all can! An ever fluctuating, changing, and, most precisely, a shifting back-and-forth class has money. (Not wealth.) And whoever has the money sets the tone, at the film premieres and in the bars where they dance naked (or as good as), in low, leather-upholstered cars, in hotels, and wine bars. Rich people are only tolerable as a phenomenon when the spirit of the money—*olet! olet!*—has become a little blurred. Written on every forehead here: Moolah! Blatant and brutal and with a little honest desire for dictatorship. (Which we actually have, without a single soul complaining.) I'll never forget the fat man seated in a large hall in the Esplanade—at a large table laden with coffee, sugar, milk, and pastries. "Yes," he said, stuffing a whole doughnut into his mouth. "Look, as for Bolshevism ... those people don't work!" At least he worked.

Women are mirrors. Riches ruin those women who are always with the winners in life. Those words recently uttered in the provinces by a brave prosecutor, concerning the bourgeois beguilers of working women, were a bit overstated—but most of it was true. And so easy to understand. A little glitter at night, not always gray, a little music and wine and sparkle ... and bye-bye, beloved homeland ... Plötzensee.*

And right next door—the stink of poverty. Just a little way beyond the middle classes, who complain, caught up with old notions and still unable to believe that their time has passed—right next door, in the working-class Gesundbrunnen district, in the East, in the North, is a poverty that seems all the more terrible because of all the efforts to keep it from being visible on the streets. No begging allowed! "The German homes in Berlin's slums are all wearing tux fronts," Count Kessler once said. All show ... But inside?

Inside it's like a returning prisoner of war once told me, "I was in Siberia for five years, where they kept telling us how miserable Russian life is. But here—" He gestured around his pathetic room, in which seven people, male and female, had to bunk together. "Look at this! This is much worse! And no one helps us!" The saddest part is that the people who *work* live like that. What about the unemployed? They become animals. Because a nation doesn't go down like an ironclad warship. It gets lice.

What's really strange is the hatred the rich have for the poor, especially for the workers. What was once compassion—sentimental,

---

* T. is referring to a recent court case in the city of Görlitz: a woman was acquitted after stabbing her boyfriend, an army officer who had left her. The judge believed that "those bourgeois classes see working girls as objects of their lust." Plötzensee is a large prison in Berlin.

useless compassion—is now pure hatred. Mixed with fear. Will they do something to us along the Kurfürstendamm? Thank God we still have the city's Security Brigade!

This oft-maligned city, unloved in the provinces, hated for all the wrong reasons (others rarely see our true faults)—this city is less united than ever. It lives on, just like old times, in picture books and operettas: with whistling cobblers' apprentices, fat, old, Weissbier-drinking Berliners, market women with mouths yapping a mile a minute … Everything, all of it has grown harsher, and that utterly Berlin sense of humor (Berliners always told their best and most biting jokes in the morning, before they'd had anything to eat)—that's gone. Just a glimmer sometimes. Standing room only on the trains, and everything so full that people can hardly breathe. A garbage truck drives by, and the driver grins, "Hey, why doncha take a seat?"

And as long as they're still really Berliners, that old idiosyncrasy is still evident, of not letting themselves be fooled, suspecting a con, resenting big words. "My place?—OK." And the other one can beat it.

Does this city have a face? What is it? Is it still that dreadful, unwavering, German "efficiency" of which the office clerk is the ideal representation? (The Ameronger was just such a clerk, in uniform.)*

Shouldn't it go beyond the ability to run the shop? The clothing and movie industries have an intrinsic affinity. One thing sets the standard for everything else: success. As Carl Sternheim notes with self-loathing in his new book, *Berlin*, it affects this city, which is always inclined to start over again—always sticking to the facts. The city lives. Will it still be alive tomorrow?

There's a subway car. The sign says "Berlin." It's jam-packed, so full that a window creaks, and this man is standing on a lady's big toe. He says, "I jus' wanna tell you, Missy, what you can do—you can jus' kiss … nuthin', that's what!" Where will this lead?

We're all sitting inside and we don't have a clue. Train's leaving!

---

* T. liked to ridicule Wilhelm II as the "Ameronger" because after World War I and the 1918 Revolution, the Emperor fled to Amerongen Castle in the Netherlands where he signed his abdication from the throne. The revolution ended in August 1919 with the formation of the Weimar Republic.

Tucholsky's birthplace, at 13 Lübecker Strasse in Berlin-Moabit. **Above left:** *The Kindergarten within the building is named "Tiger, Panther & Co.," after his pseudonyms and one of his books.* **Above right:** *A plaque commemorates the author.* **Right:** *The gallery, also within the building, was named "Kurt."*

Interview with Myself

Peter Panter, Berliner Tageblatt, September 3, 1919

"Mr. Panter will see you now!" the servant said.

I stepped forward.

The tall door to the boss's office opened. The servant held the curtain to the side—I walked through, and the door closed behind me.

The huge man sat at his desk—you might even say he was fat. He wore the well-groomed look of an autocrat, though his multiple chins sort of ruined the effect. His hair stuck straight up like a stiff brush, and his beady eyes reflected comfort and fulfillment. He stood up.

"Welcome, young man," he said. "Have a seat and tell me about your strange letter!"

Feeling uneasy, I sat down.

"You asked me," the boss said, and he placed his fat hand with the well-manicured nails in such a way that I couldn't help noticing them, "if I could advise you about your future. You mentioned that you're determined to achieve some grand ideal. You keep bumping up against life, which seems 'sharply edged' to you—that was the phrase you used—and you'd like my advice. Well, young man, I can certainly give you some."

I bowed in gratitude.

"First," the boss said. "What do you do for a living?"

"Nothing at all," I admitted, feeling ashamed of myself.

"Hmm," the boss remarked, shaking his head solemnly. "Not much to go on. Still ... I'm at your service."

"Sir," I said, mustering up some courage, "Teach me how to succeed. How did you succeed? Achieve all this?" I gestured around the comfortably furnished room—gilded, vellum-bound books arranged on big shelves, a bronze floor lamp glowing with a soft, subdued light, and the expensive ashtray of black-veined marble on the desk before me. "How did you come to this?" I asked.

The boss smiled oddly.

"Success? You want to know the secret to my success, young man? You young fool! I submitted."

"I could never do that—never!" I cried emphatically.

"You have to," he said. "You will. What did you do during the war?"

"I was …" I mumbled, looking at the tips of my boots. "I dug trenches."

"Wrong!" he said. "If you were a clever lad, with experience, you would have been somewhere else—in a press office, or with the political police or something. Don't you know anything about compromise? Are you capable of making concessions?"

"Never!" I shouted.

"You'll have to. They'll make you. Look at me—these are the sweet spoils of compromise. You have to get on in life, my young friend!"

"But what about truth? What about ideals?" I shouted, louder than was appropriate. "What about the things that make life worth living? I'm still a Sturm-und-Dranger, and I'm going to stay that way! I'll call a murder murder, even if someone waves a flag over it; an opportunist an opportunist, even if he's some power-hungry bureaucrat; and an old boys' network an old boys' network, even if the whole town stands behind it! That's what I want to do! Help me! Show me how to achieve that, for my own salvation, and for what I believe to be the sake of all mankind!"

I had worked myself up; my cheeks glowed red-hot, and my lips were parted and trembling.

The boss smiled. The big boss Peter Panter smiled.

"My dear young man," he said, with emphasis. "Listen carefully to what I'm saying. I understand your noble sentiments, which do you such credit. I, too, wish that man were as noble as you make him out to be. I, too, I dare say, represent all that is good, true, and beautiful. And I love all that is good, true, and beautiful—indeed, I adore it. But, my dear young friend, real life gets in the way! You have to face reality, figure out when bending is prudent, or even necessary …"

"I don't want to submit," I interrupted him stubbornly.

"You will submit. You'll have to submit. One day you'll want to earn money, and you'll submit. It's so easy—so sweet—to give in a little—a slight nod, a tiny renunciation of principle, and suddenly you're a beloved, respected, well-received young man! Isn't that what you want?"

I shook my head contemptuously.

"Now, now," the boss soothed. "Think about what you're doing! You'll want to marry, start a family, a home—and you'll submit. What good to you or anyone else will those principles be, that rigid adherence to the truth, or what you call truth? On the other hand, you'll see—what does it cost me? I'm friendly to everyone; I say 'yes' to everyone, while you might indignantly say 'no.' And I know when to hold my tongue. Silence doesn't cost a thing—the finest jewel in the crown of human arts.* Shut up!"

"I must speak!" I shouted.

"No, you mustn't. No one must! Shut up. Submit! Submit to money and submit to praise; submit to power—to that above all—and submit to women. And what will be your reward?"

He leaned back in his chair and smiled smugly.

"As you can see," he continued, "I live comfortably, and I'm quite satisfied. Priests and doctors, officers and artists congregate in my home—no one is insulted by my writing, and everyone gets a bottle of good red wine. Do you really think I don't see what's behind all this? It just doesn't concern me. They read my work and they buy my books—what more could I want? Is it my job to tell them the truth, the hard, uncomfortable truth?"

"It's everyone's job to tell humanity the truth!" I said.

"Not mine," the boss said. "Not mine. I quit that job, and I've done quite well ever since. And since then I've had everything I need—even more than I need. My daughter will soon be marrying a factory owner. Yes, indeed."

"Should I get married?" I asked.

"Not to the woman you love—I'm guessing she doesn't have any money. Marry a rich man's daughter. There's room in even the smallest mansion—but it must be a mansion. Do you smoke?"

---

* A reference to *Wilhelm Meister's Apprenticeship*, a novel by Johann Wolfgang von Goethe. The remark at the bottom of the page that there is "room is even in the smallest mansion," is a reference to a poem by Friedrich Schiller, "There is room enough in the smallest hut for a happy, loving pair."

The author in 1908, at age eighteen, posing as "Ignaz Wrobel," one of his four pseudonyms, in a photographer's studio.

"No," I replied, "I don't smoke. I …"

"Smoke!" he said genially. "It settles you down. And listen to what I say—because I'm standing at the top of that ladder you want to climb. Success is everything. There are four ways to achieve it: through compromise, keeping your mouth shut, listening, and flattering the old boys. If you understand that, you've got it made! And it's so great to have it made!"

His smile was greasy, like a mime's after the applause.

I stood up and gave him an angry, dubious look.

"You're fighting me on this today," Peter Panter said. "But in thirty years, you won't anymore. Make sure it's not too late then. Fare thee well, and take care!"

I shook the hand he offered and stormed out.

In the office, seated at his ostentatious desk, the boss shook his head and smiled. "Young people these days," he said. "Bashing their heads against the walls and smarter than all the rest of us. Still, we've all got to experience it for ourselves. Now I'd like some tea! Franz!"

And he rang the bell.

Outside, I stood at the fence, the cast-iron handle of the park gate in my hand, quaking with hate, wracked with rage, powerless, venomous, and feeling like the guy might have been right, at least from his point of view.

"What a disgusting man," I said.

Part II
Before the Great War:
The Gilded Age

Fairy Tale

Der Ulk, *November 22, 1907*

Once upon a time, there was an emperor who ruled over a vast, rich, and beautiful land. Like every other emperor, he had a treasure chamber, and in it, amidst all his glittering, gleaming jewels, was a flute. But this was a strange instrument. If you happened to look into one of the four holes in the flute—oh, the things you would see! There was an entire landscape inside, small but full of life: a landscape à la Thomas, with clouds by Böcklin and lakes by Leistikow. Rezniçekian little ladies wrinkled their noses at Zillean characters in there, and a Meunierian peasant lass held an armful of Orlík flowers. In short, the whole modern movement was arrayed inside the flute. And what did the emperor do with the flute? He blew it off.*

---

* Hans Thoma, Arnold Böcklin, Walter Leistikow, Ferdinand von Rezniçek, Heinrich Zille, Constantin Meuniers, and Emil Orlik were modern artists, photographers, and painters of which the rather conservative Kaiser did not approve.

Harun al-Rashid

tu, Vorwärts, *July 11, 1912*

A Berlin police chief, like that illustrious caliph Harun al-Rashid, had the habit of dressing in humble clothing and walking in the city among his people, so he could hear firsthand the opinions and complaints of the common man. One day he happened to be standing by a horse trough when he heard some coachmen indulging in unseemly words—as such people are wont to do—concerning the laws and regulations pertaining to the art of driving horses, and vigorously vilifying the same. Along came Harun al-Jagof, who expressed his opinion that the supplicants' complaints were undoubtedly based on exaggeration. A man from the group approached him and said, "Lemme tell ya somethin'. Why don'cha get yerself up on a box an' drive, an' I'll sit inside, and we'll just see what happens." So the illustrious Harun al-Rashid did just that, and sure enough, during the half-hour drive he was written up for 71 transgressions against the police's cab-drivers' ordinance. Astonished (yet ever mindful of his noble heritage), he turned to the driver reclining in the back seat of the cab and exclaimed, "Well, now I see. But tell me, is there anyone among you who actually understands the provisions contained in this ordinance?"

"The horses," replied the man of the people. *

---

* T. wrote this story after he was told that the police commissioner in the East Prussian city of Koenigsberg had insisted that police hand out as many traffic tickets as possible. Harun al-Jagof is a wordplay on Harun al-Rashid, the Persian Kalif who listened to the commoners in disguise, and Traugott von Jagow, the police commissioner in post-WWI Berlin.

Berlin Cabaret

Kurt Tucholsky, Die Schaubühne, March 6, 1913

At the piano: Rudolf Nelson. The rocking, sliding, coquettish refrains of the songs "bubble" over the keys, his fingers barely moving, but then, when the chorus comes around again (ritardando ... in print there's a fermata), you can feel his delight in the beat, in its light, pleasant rhythm. With him at the piano, you understand the meaning and the importance of a song's chorus.

At center stage: Miss Erlholz. She is one of the four people in the Berlin cabaret scene who, detached from the disreputable trappings of their occupation, have some genuine quality. With the "subtlety" of a doorman's daughter, her job in Berlin is to appear elegant and gently but firmly to present—without forcing or exaggerating or making a caricature of herself—the whole brash give-and-take of late-night entertainment with the same cold composure one might show a non-paying john.[*]

Or at center stage: a small black guy with cherry-red lips, nimble as a dancer and coquettish as a goldfinch. But this androgynous fashion-addict is thoroughly intolerable: what Vadasz once portrayed in a number from *Assiette au Beurre* ("Les petit jeunes hommes")—those limber Italian boys, for whom concepts like sin, perversion, and the renunciation of Philistinism simply don't exist, because they're essentially promiscuous little pigs—even that would be acceptable. But this other one, sure, he's good at what he does, easily laying down a dainty, punctuated, pizzicato refrain, a lilting dance, and there are moments when he comically parodies a groan (the way he says the word "perfume" is like throwing an orgy)—but once he leaves the stage, you're left with a slightly schmaltzy impres-

---

[*] T. refers to a number of artists from the Roaring Twenties. Rudolf Nelson was a composer, and the founder and director of the cabaret troupe *Nelson Revue*. Käthe Erlholz, a singer, was his wife. Miklos Vadasz was a Hungarian artist; he drew cartoons for the satirical monthly *L'Assiette au Beurre*.

sion, a bad aftertaste, like something wasn't quite finished. Franz Blei comments on Aubrey Beardsley, "Sin becomes beautiful and virtuous, because it's large and commanding, and the little sin that fights with the little virtue for supremacy within an individual becomes repulsively ugly."*

These are just a few. The rest shuffle across the stage—semi-talented, making noise, some funny, but lacking ideas and personality. None that don't grovel before the audience, no direction deemed anything beyond an assignment, their bawdiness designed to get the shady developers and noncommissioned officers to drink more and more champagne. Dirty jokes ... here's the thing about us: we stop where the French are just getting started. Analysis of these cabaret songs does confirm the existence of extramarital sex, though these comic problems are not elaborated here—the hostile husband and wife, and this broad, and that broad, "and what happened next. . ." The performer winks, and the audience understands and hollers in ready and worthy anticipation. . . nothing more.

Miss Waldoff. If she doesn't get fat, that consummate Berlin boyish gamine, that cobbler's apprentice type that smug playboy-shopboys flock to in young women these days. The type is getting more and more common ... she stands there, arms hanging down (something she learned how to do), satisfied expression (she learned that, too), singing (something she hasn't learned yet). Her technique is impossible and inimitable, inimitable, like Girardi's: hundreds try to copy it, so you might say a new style has emerged, but no one even comes close. Who stands there like she does, head tilted slightly back and to the side, one eyebrow raised, the left corner of her mouth pulled down? "My Berlin is one cool town!" she says, decked out in that sleek black dress with its white folded collar, and she makes a rude bow like a young boy. Maybe that's the pinnacle of humor, transcending everything so coolly and impassively, and contemptuously dismissing it all as the incarnation of indifference. Just listen to the way she says the

---

* Aubrey Beardsley was an nineteenth century English illustrator. Félix Mayol was a French entertainer. Franz Blei was a German author. Alexander Girardi (mentioned further below on this page) was an Austrian actor.

Claire Waldoff, born Clara Wortmann, was a famed chanteuse of the 1920 and 1930s, and also after World War II. She lived in Berlin with her American-born girlfriend, Olga von Roeder; the couple was the center of Berlin's lesbian community in the Roaring Twenties.

word "springtime," glancing down to the side, flushing hundreds of sentiments down the drain. She doesn't even make an effort; she clinically pronounces her fans "crrr-razy," and people believe her; there's no detectable undercurrent of secret joy about what an effect she still has on men! We forget, with this slightly derisive performance, that it's about one of the two great pillars on which, according to Schiller, the world rests ... humor is a contrasting effect. She approaches matters coolly that would make others' heads, legs, and wallets spin, noting with a shake of her head like God Almighty on his throne, "When the groom and the bride ..." She is so *Berlin* you can't tell for sure whether she isn't really shy deep down and her superiority isn't sheer sauciness; the refrains glide over her flapper-lips, and with her contemptuously hunched shoulders, she's the grotesque image of cheeky maidenhood: "Keep your hands to yourself, pleeeeease ..." Therein lies her primary appeal: Jokes, sharp one-liners that drift off in smoke. Wordplay, witticism ... Impossible.

Once it was about a virgin who tried to electrocute herself in Potsdamer Square. It was a strange situation—they censored her punch line. I can still see it now: she sang some harmless nonsense instead, eyes rolled impudently upward so we could see their bluish whites, grinning mischievously at the audience, her innocence secure, as far as she was concerned; she remained an unwritten page, wholly blameless for the lack of a punch line. But it was so much cheekier than the first time. And the memory of a dark-colored U remains, a consonant oozing from the depths of a constricted throat, pinched, squeezed, and the mocking, malicious glee with which she dismissed the little cadet, the bride, John Doe, and the rest of us:

" ... and didn't make it in the end,
No, lovin' ain't so easy"

But there are printed versions of Mayol's lieder: the chansonnier smiling saucily on the cover, with an upturned curl, one hand visible, accompanying on the keys: *Hou! Les femmes!**

And no one in Berlin can do that.

---

* Wow! Those Ladies!

Summertime in Berlin

Peter Panter, Die Schaubühne, August 28, 1913

The blinds are drawn. Peter Panter sits alone in the room. Outside, it's bright summer, with white specks fluttering down onto empty streets; the sky is a clear pastel blue, and the sun ... the sun—what a town! Only now, with everyone gone, do you begin to feel the hustle and bustle they all took with them, all that restless agitation. Everything seems to have adopted a softer pace—the streetcars and the newspapers and the ones left behind.

Yes, there's a theater, too. You might not think it possible, but it's true. The Wannsee is there, along with many other lakes in Mark Brandenburg, glittering in the sun, the wind blowing softly through the tall plants along the shores. One does not exclude the other. God ordained it so—in the city they're putting on a show. Some still, some again, and some have never really stopped.

On the kiosks, among sleepy advertisements for Lanolin and Gent la, the new three-penny cigarette, one is shouting: Sylvester Schäffer!!! The greatest artistic genius of all time!!! Who said that? The Impresario—no, really, make that "Impresa" S. Rachmann, which promptly brings to mind—as the names demand—adenoids, thick palatal sounds, snorting at the dinner table, and a long, drawn-out "Peee-ewww"!! The boy does a lot but isn't really good at much.[*]

But here in the big city, we've lost so much more: our desire, wide expanses, and the clouds—we see them only in bits and pieces, and then not at all—and all that stuff. We've lost tranquillity.

So, the way you live now, subscribers, is how you should live all year long—quietly, gently, thoughtfully. Then things take on a differ-

---

[*] In this piece, T. mocks Berlin moguls and wannabes in the 1920s movie business. Sylvester Schäffer was a vaudeville artist, dancer, painter, violinist and magician who emigrated to Hollywood in 1935 and was soon forgotten. Sam Rachmann was the buying agent for the German film studio UFA in New York; he nearly wrecked the studio with his million-dollar deals.

ent complexion; the sea teaches us to smile, where we once were angry; the mountains show us how small things are, which once seemed so big; and when the wind begins to blow, nothing can bother us.

Right—you'd like to? Well, you can.

Almost all of us are forced to stay in this big city because we need to make a living. But we should slow down that hectic pace that ruins the better and repels the best of us, to a more humane pace. It's not even American—for that we have neither the strength nor the ruthlessness—the whole thing just acts like a village gone crazy. It's still just a small town that must first grow into the clothes set out for it by the shady developers. And that will take a while.

In the meantime, they're building one cinema after another and stand anxiously at the cash registers, wondering how it will all turn out. Will it? Not that way.

The Herrnfelds' wriggle by on the movie screens, and the people laugh a little—in the brothers' own theater, they even roar with laughter. But there's no cowboy drama afterward to bring tears to their eyes, so they yawn instead.

They have to leave. Outside, in Potsdamer Square, they're playing a song in the "Grand-Luxur-Gala-Palace-Café," or whatever that thing is called, and all of the dishwashing maids cry along, a folk-song-butchering tune. And yet summer is everywhere, with mild air and a little of that happy tranquillity that is otherwise utterly lacking in this city.

---

* Donat and Anton Herrnfeld were brothers, actors, and vaudevillians well known in prewar Berlin.

The Policed

Anonymous, Vorwärts, September 18, 1913

There's a Berlin streetcar … Probably not much different from other streetcars … People are sitting there and daydreaming and staring and talking to each other, and some are reading … Suddenly a man in uniform enters the car and says, "Tickets, please!" He's an official whose primary function is to check everyone's ticket.

Dutifully, everyone digs in his pocket. Everyone hands the official a piece of paper. But one man has lost his ticket.

The German people are definitely a subservient bunch. Now they're all looking at the man, as if he's committed some crime. Because they imagine that the official is inspecting them. The official is polite and not actually doing anything that might support this suspicion. But that's what they think, and they're quite frightened, and they actually loathe the man who lost his ticket. In one instant, the entire car has turned against him. Maybe one person, watching him struggle, feels a little sympathy, even shudders to imagine himself in such a dreadful situation …

They cower. Their faces turn red. The loser's face turns dark red. He apologizes. He does not say, "I misplaced it, I'd be happy to pay now …" He feels caught. Suddenly the man before them isn't considered an adult, maybe with a wife, kids to raise, employees to boss around … Here he's just small. Because the most sacred German of all has arrived: the uniform. The joke stops here.

A trivial matter, for sure, nothing of consequence. Just another simple observation from daily life, which shows how an individual here doesn't dare say, "Hello! Here I am!" Instead his face turns red, and he cowers and looks for his ticket.

And that's one of the hardships of German life.

Berlin Is Having Fun!

Anonymous, Vorwärts, October 10, 1913

Yet another entertainment palace has opened on Potsdamer Street. A palace ... but it costs thirty cents to get in. And there's the rub: the name clashes with the reality. What's inside? Noise. Not natural noise, which gets drunk on itself—the happy hubbub of happy people—but corporate noise. The blaring kind you pay for. Bands. Lots of bands. A horse track. A dance floor. A slide. Cabaret. It's all there, but none of it's right.

The Berliner feels utterly out of place there: he wanders through the din, slightly bored, taking it all in, graciously, not necessarily opposed to allowing himself to be entertained. But not much comes of it. Because he brings nothing but his wallet, and just like that joyful exclamation—Yahoo!—that he borrowed from southern Germany, he scrounges up all manner of *joie de vivre* wherever he can find it, from Bavaria, Tirol—anywhere but Berlin. Because the Berliner shed his own simple skin long ago and was forced to take up foreign ways by the clever businessmen who knew which button to push— his vanity—and behold: a fool in the eyes of the world. Berlin is having fun.

But something different, and gloomier, is apparent when you observe a spectacle like this Odéon—the intersection of Berlin's petty bourgeoisie and its underworld. Clerks and shopgirls go from one "establishment" to the next, where they spend more money than they earn in a week. No organization could recruit them—but this is what they're all about. They're an entirely different breed from those who employ the educational tools at their disposal, who care about better pay and go after it—but those who behave this way are not small in number. They all inflate themselves; no one's content with who he is; they all aspire to a higher level. Berlin is having fun ...

Carnival in Berlin

Theobald Tiger, Die Schaubühne, February 12, 1914

Now the Berliner spits in his hand
and gets to work on having a ball,
slaving away from start to end
throughout this Carnival time.

Suddenly a call from the heights
of cosmopolitan elegance
along the Spree and canals, delights,
"Put on your escarpins and dance!"

This mood, indeed, this very Muse,
naturally all men does stain;
the hand, by day to satin used,
casually beckons for champagne.

In her own way, the lady carnivals,
license granted once each year,
smooching strictly in closed circles,
when all competition is far from here.

The middle class soul is infected too,
and keeps the dark beer flowing,
joyfully hollering, "Yahoo!"
bag o'er head in colors glowing.

What even wise men hold more dear
than thoughts sublime is wine!
Thus filled, he goes to see his Claire,*
Berlin dins, he smiles …
To thee be thine.

---

*   "Claire" was what Tucholsky called his first wife, Else Weil.

Kurt Tucholsky

At the Movies

wr., Vorwärts, December 12, 1913

The cinema on Nollendorfplatz is running a lukewarm lineup. One really should give up on those ever-awful Italian films: no one wants to see that garish, pompous stuff anymore. Apart from that, it's strange how everything in the world is moving forward except for the cinema. It's still the same as it was two or three years ago—nothing, absolutely nothing has changed. Still the same inanity, the same technical and artistic mistakes—and yet the finest are still those large railway trains rolling silently toward us without a sound, making us jump back, and then disappearing again …

At the very end: "America–Europe by Airship." The concept is bad Jules Verne. One man follows a woman from America across the ocean to Europe, on to St. Petersburg, and then drags her back to America. Good. But if you don't have the money to produce decent shots, you shouldn't bother at all. The American hotel was the Esplanade on Bellevuestrasse in Berlin, and the New York Harbor was a stretch along the Spree River near a factory, with apple barges bobbing peacefully on the water and only a Negro and an American police uniform representing the foreign continent. The millionaires all appeared to be in desperate need of an advance on their next month's wages, which let's hope the film company granted them, and the dance hall in St. Petersburg was indistinguishable from one of your better hoedowns, with all due respect. Only …

Only the leading role was played by Germany's strongest cabaret figure, so the film is relatively interesting to watch. But oh, how inept those film people are! They filmed Gussy Holl, a natural profile, from the front often enough, with unflattering results, and they didn't even understand how to put her delightful gestures to good use (like that typical Berlin nose stuck in the air with the head at an angle: "Bah! What can you do to me?") This great artist, whose impact lies in the details, was dragged from the boat to the balloon and later, in the indoor scenes, no director was there at all, just some guy rolling the film. A couple of nice balloon shots couldn't make up for the rest. And were I to pass the selfsame way hundreds of years from yonder day, they still won't have figured out how to take good shots or correctly frame a pearl like Miss Holl.

Above: Mary Gerold, Tucholsky's second wife and the love of his life. *Right*: The actress Auguste "Gussy" Holl, whom the author adored, with Tucholsy.

The Monitors

Vorwärts, March 17, 1914

When I look out my window, across the street, I see the red brick front of a neighborhood school in Berlin. In summer, when it's warm, and in spring, too, we both—the district school and I—open our windows. Then I can hear fifty-three children's voices confirming they're Prussian and even want to be Prussian, and I hear them offering up hymns to God Almighty, all day long, without ceasing, such that the old man will probably soon think that Prussia is just one giant nursery.

But it's the most delightful there at 10 and 11 o'clock, in short, whenever recess comes to an end. Then the classes wait for their teachers to return, and with fifty kids together in one room, there's nothing quiet about it. There's one class, behind the first windows on the left, third floor, filled with loud little girls who make such a fuss until Mr. Teacher enters the room, or Miss Teacher, to teach them their advanced multiplication tables and basic needlecrafts. And because everything on earth requires order these days, a pair of monitors, maybe the best pupils in class, are assigned to stand at the podium and make sure that the unruly swarm doesn't get too loud.

And it's really strange, but at that time, at 10 o'clock or 11 o'clock, I barely hear a thing from the unruly class, save two clear, screeching voices, always the same, so I recognize them, shouting, "Quiet! Be quiet! You're supposed to be quiet! Silence! Quiet!" And from the entire class, this is all I hear: Quiet. Silence. The others really are still and silent, and only the monitors continue to sniff out the rebels and call, in their highest sopranos, for decent behavior …

But as far as German politics are concerned, I'll keep my mouth shut.

Part III
After the Great War:
The Weimar Republic

Berlin's Gambling Dens

Ignaz Wrobel, Berliner Tageblatt, March 20, 1919

The "little ponies" that southern Europeans allow to run in their lands, gambling casinos, are forbidden in Germany. But the people's lust for such games tempers pressure from above, and the police bust up only the bare minimum necessary to generate publicity for such state institutions, so that enough of them can and do survive.

As a result, the prohibition hasn't done much. When the seductions of gambling entrepreneurs are shut out of the town squares, amusement parks, and theater lobbies, there's a big impact. But between public and private life, a semipublic life has emerged—everyone gets in, or at least whoever wants to. And who wants to?

Not just the shady folks. That's the big difference between Berlin before the war and Berlin today; the unreliability of these hybrid classes has eaten its way deep into the bourgeoisie. It's not just those crooks in black tails and white ties who used to strut on the sheets of street artists back then and strut on the cinema screen today, to the dismay of all right-minded citizens. Today the right-minded citizens are playing their hearts out too.

But it's really a shame. Unlike that Licentiate Mumm,* we don't suspect that every big city is a morass (heavenward gaze) of human

---

* Friedrich Mumm was a pastor, and a parliamentarian of the Deutschnationale Volkspartei (German National People's Party) who ran on an anti-smut ticket.

vices, a den of iniquity, my dears, that God would smite. We know very well that in the big city, like everywhere else, social circumstances determine that some work because they must, some laze about because they can, and a third group wheels and deals because the ground here is ripe for black marketeering. So it would be a big mistake to pin this new phenomenon of wild Berlin gambling dens on the visitors and toot the horn for morality when an entirely different tune is being played. So, what's really going on here?

The players in the big Berlin clubs used to be traders, actors, attorneys, people with completely solid bourgeois livelihoods, for whom the games were one of life's pleasures and an indispensable bonus. Today, people gamble in some fifty to eighty newly established casinos in western Berlin. For those who want to play, it's not difficult to gain admission, so these clubs can be considered essentially public. The stakes are high, by middle-class standards, the turnover extraordinary, and the operators' profits very good. The decor in the clubs is elegant—a touch of that fresh Berlin elegance—but it does cost money; they offer plenty of inexpensive food—no thanks to the Office against Wartime Profiteering and its successors—and champagne and wine, after all, are merely drops on the hot stones in the women's jewelry. So far, so good.

What I find alarming about the situation is that the public that frequents these casinos isn't entirely solid, and the unsound element hiding in every player has infected the previously respectable bourgeoisie. It's tempting: the night life is so easy and elegant and tempting, nerves firing, itching for action, and hot eyes welcome a gray day—a day, but not a work day. The fact that only the operators really profit, and the waiters, the meat delivery men—what does the player care? He's looking for something totally different from profits. The true player doesn't play for the money—he's drawn to the green table, the swishing shuffle of the cards, the rush, the atmosphere of greed, envy, and restless agitation buzzing around the table … Money? Bah!

The Berlin bourgeoisie has not remained immune to this disease. They play even where the late Fontane[*] chatted over orange salad; they play at ladies' teas and men's stag parties; they play at home and

---

[*] Theodor Fontane was a nineteeth-century Berlin novelist.

away from home. Rampant neglect of manners has spread, the likes of which wasn't even seen in the less than stable Berlin of the first few years of the century. Everything was uncertain and unsteady then, so much was still new and incomplete—the good old Berlin only existed in a few streets, crumbling blocks replaced by stucco—and yet a certain industrious solidarity among the bourgeoisie couldn't be denied. What happened to that? We look back on those years of peace almost wistfully, when business morals in every decent company were so high that they didn't want to have anything to do with gamblers and opportunists. And today?

Today the number of long-standing honest merchants is dwindling. This began when people began taking on war deliveries they didn't understand, which they negotiated and traded back and forth, like the Galician trader with his basket that could hold whatever the cadres needed: dachshunds, suspenders, and lampshades. Ridiculous war profits followed, goods practically given away, supplies stockpiled, speculation fraught with politics and artificially induced booms and busts. And peace came to be not a cry for salvation by the downtrodden, but a sad confirmation of the fact that from now on chocolate stocks would fall substantially ...

What's easily earned is easily spent. Those who work like that amuse themselves accordingly and one day will no longer want to work at all. Values are skewed: a barber at a casino on Bellevuestrasse earns 10,000 marks a year for unrumpling the men who live right there in the club, after their long nights. And the bourgeoisie doesn't turn away. The police shouldn't take care of it for them; whoever wants to fall can fall—there are enough paragraphs in Germany. That's not how to deal with it. There's an intellectual culture above the casino—people don't avoid gambling because they find it amoral, but because they find it stupid. Yet the bourgeoisie doesn't turn away. This is not to say that every better family runs a roulette table now, but the broad middle class's aversion to the endeavor is not as great as it should be to isolate the clubs. Today's good, honest citizens: how long will they stay that way, with that kind of life?

What we're missing isn't a new caste or class arrogance; we have more than enough of that and will still have enough after the officer has disappeared from the social scene. What we're missing is the natural fighting spirit that says, "I'm a merchant, no more, no less. Not a knight, not a professor, 'just' a merchant. But I'm holding my shield in my hand, and my shield is pure." Now there are more and more people here who can show us a clean shop sign, but that's about it …

Is Purgatory roiling in Berlin's gambling dens? The poor souls, worn down by the long years of wartime suffering, drunk from the gold- and profit-mongering of the war, they flutter like moths to the flame. Let them fall. Just make sure that the rest of us, those who remain above, regard the ones below as what they are: social parasites of decent society.

Potsdamer Platz, Berlin's premier nightlife location, in the 1930s.

We Really Should Have ...

Peter Panter, Berliner Tageblatt, October 2, 1919

Alexander Moszkowski* once described a family's feelings after a big summer trip; in his description, each sentence began with the words, "We really should have ... We really should have left on Friday; we really should have gone over the Brenner Pass; we really should have left the big suitcase at home." And it ended with, "We really should have stayed at home!"

We really should have ... that's something to consider. When I tap it out on the piano of my thoughts, my typewriter, it resonates for a long while—almost like a theme that can be played with many variations. We really should have ...

When the three of us, Karlchen, Jakopp and I, were traveling up from Romania, back when the Great War was winding down, we came one night to the Hungarian station of Szolnog. There was a fork in the road: we could go to Budapest along the Panke or through Bohemia. Now what? In Bohemia, we'd heard, there was revolt and rebellion, but the other way wasn't any safer ... We went by way of Pest and made it home. But of all that commotion, the red-wine nights in the private compartment, the young Romanian officer who looked like a Berlin bartender, the many colorful schnapps in the big bathhouse in Pest, from Salzburg to Munich—out of all that, Karlchen didn't remember a thing. Whenever I see him these days, he shakes his head dejectedly and says reproachfully, "We really should have changed trains in Szolnog!"

Really? Would things have been any different? There are those who claim their entire lives would have been different if they'd changed trains in Szolnog—and they're the same people who, afterward, when

---

* Alexander Moszkowski was a German satirist of Polish-Jewish descent. He was the brother of the musician Moritz Moszkowski, who was the music teacher of Mark Twain's daughter Clara Clemens when the family lived in Berlin.

everything is over, are terribly clever and tell us what we should have done but didn't, and how everything might have turned out if only …

I don't really believe those people. I can't help suspecting that the gift of seeing the situation after the fact, of knowing how things should have been done, is an evil gift—no one really learns anything from it.

We really should have … Once I went out with Auguste; it was a pleasant Saturday evening; she wore her best dress, relatively new boots, and looked awfully elegant. I didn't dare address her by her first name … And we sat in the best seat in the theater, proscenium box left—the theater was on Grosse Frankfurter Strasse—and we saw *Twice Raped, or: The Freemason's Love*. It was terribly exciting. Auguste interrupted the play with adept comments, and it took all of my skill to avoid being thrown out. The hero was put in some kind of coal container, which on that night was standing in for a coffin; the heroine crashed a freemasons' meeting, full of serious men who weren't playing cards, but were chanting sinister spells instead, because the hero was supposed to be inducted; the prompter got caught up in the ceremony and whispered so softly that the actors got stuck—and Auguste was so moved, she snuffled in my handkerchief. And when it was all over and the knot tied, after the catastrophe and the finale with the two couples and the distraught extras and the applause and the curtain going up and down—"Well?" I asked.

And Auguste said, "We really should have gone to see *The Hunter from Kurpfalz*"—women are seldom grateful.

We really should have … There are people who say it at the end of a marriage that has lasted decades, and there are those who say it to themselves after they've carefully considered everything and made an important decision. People often say it after a trip or after they've decided not to have some wild, frivolous fun. People can't really help themselves.

It's an entire philosophy, this "We really should have …"—a cheap, entertaining, and incontrovertible philosophy. Doesn't everything turn out wonderfully when you rewrite it later? You took the path to

---

* *The Hunter from Kurpfalz* is a rather racy folk song. The play *Twice Raped* … is most likely fictional.

the right, and you experienced difficulty and sorrow and bitter disappointment. But the path to the left, the one you really should have taken, was smooth sailing! Our thoughts gently drift to those places where everything bends to our will, without inhibitions and catastrophes—that path would have been free of hurdles, it would have led straight to the goal. We really should have …

Sometimes it's also a thorn in our sides; indeed, there are women who can make an entire porcupine out of the phrase. Everything was very nice: the rest of us drank red wine and danced and kissed a little bit—which happened at an unguarded moment—and chatted. "Well, Mama, how was it?" "It was really nice, my boy. But I got so angry—Papa ordered creamed schnitzel, and later I saw the menu and noticed that there was a cheaper schnitzel … two marks wasted … He really should have … !" But it must be said that there are also such women among men. Once we were traveling over the Hungarian-Romanian border, to Orsova. I'll spare myself the grief and won't mention the alcohol—but it was beautiful. The first lieutenant didn't have enough Hungarian currency and paid with his Romanian leis, and naturally got cheated on the exchange; we took off. On the way back, we went through the tall Pappelallee—the sky stretched green overhead, the stars shining dimly through, dusk settled over the mountains, and city lights twinkled in the distance. We could hear the Danube rushing below us when the coachman let the horses rest for a while. We were silent. On the seat, full of rage, mumbling quietly, furious and thoroughly insulted, the lieutenant sat and argued with the people who had taken the commission on his exchange … a commission! He blew on and on, that old beautiful song, "We really should have … !" and ruined his whole evening.

The wise man recites the saying in vain, the one an old sergeant had etched in gold on a porcelain plate hanging above his desk, "However you do it, it's wrong!" That's some consolation! Like an obstinate bass, incessantly rolling and rumbling a deep, disturbing theme: "We really should have!" We really should have given that guy a piece of our mind! We really should have sent some flowers! We really shouldn't have paid the bill! We really should have said that child wasn't ours! And finally, completely and utterly unhappy and making a clean sweep: We really should have been born a movie star!

We really should have … And Schopenhauer's old, grumpy, wrinkled face appears, with those eyes that see through everything, laughing grimly: "You really should have? Fools! Could you have?"

We nod. We've read the treatises on the freedom of the will, of course, and we know that water only bubbles when it's flowing down the hill, that it only snows when it's cold, and that grouse only do their mating dance when it's the right time—we know these things well.

And yet, and yet … When it's all over, something pounds inside us, our faces cloud over, and after good luck and bad, births, and deaths, a soft voice says, "We really should have … !"

"Karlchen" and "Jakopp" are characters that appear in some of T.'s stories. They are based on two old friends he met in the army during World War I. In the photo above, "Karlchen" (Erich Dahnel) is on the right; "Jakopp" (Hans Fritsch) is in the center; and T. is on the left.

Flouting Love

Kaspar Hauser, Die Weltbühne, October 30, 1919

Oh, Auntie Yulla, in Neu-Ruppin*
You shudder to read Berlin's atrocities
and how the ladies spread their knees,
thinking, Babylon of sin, Berlin!
And your little eyes open with lust
'cause your coffee sisters truly must. . .
hear of that couple with legs entwined ... gee,
how can that be?

Oh, Auntie Yulla, come visit the Spree.
And see this tide up close,
as I do, get a good dose.
And imagine a *chambre séparée.*
The waiter cheats. She squeals.
Violins coax them their bodies to reveal.
One more corsette, one breast more ...
What's in store?

Oh, Auntie Yulla, blasé we are not.
And yet, this market of love is tough!
He loves little boys; that one plays rough;
and him? It's pigtails that get him hot.
Themis spews her codes of morality.
Don't consider eroticism so highly.
Just stick with your bourgeois dreams,
Nothing to miss here, it seems.
Stay in your small room, Auntie dear—
What could be there?
What could ever be there?

---

* Neu-Ruppin is a small town north of Berlin. This poem is a reference to a comic song by Otto Reutter: "Uncle Fritz from Neu-Ruppin".

White Spots

Ignaz Wrobel, Berliner Volkszeitung,
December 21, 1919

On Dorotheenstrasse in Berlin, there's a building that once housed the Prussian War Academy. A strip of granite blocks runs around the base of the building, one after another, about as tall as a man.

There's something strange about those blocks; the brown granite looks lighter in many places, as if smudged with white … What could this be?

Are they whitish spots? If they're spots, they should be reddish. During the Great War, the lists of German casualties were posted there.

They hung there, changed almost daily, those terrible pages, endless lists with name after name after name … I have the very first one of those documents; the military units were still carefully noted on it; that first one listed very few dead; it's very short, list No. 1. I don't know how many appeared after that—just that there were a great many, over a thousand. One name after another, each one signifying a human life snuffed out, or someone "missing"—crossed out for the time being—or injured, or gravely maimed.

There they hung, where the white spots are now. There they hung, and hundreds of people crowded silently around them, people whose loved ones were out there somewhere, trembling, afraid to see that one name among the many thousands. What did they care about the Müllers or Schulzes or Lehmanns posted there! Let them perish, one thousand after another—if only *his* name doesn't appear! The war thrived on that attitude.

And it was because of that very attitude that the war could go on like that for four long years. If we had all stood up as one man—who knows if it would have lasted so long. Someone once told me that I didn't know how a German man could die. I know very well how.

But I also know how a German woman can cry—and I know she's still crying today, because slowly, excruciatingly slowly, she's beginning to understand what it was that he died for. For what … ?

Am I rubbing salt in old wounds? I'd rather burn holy fire in those wounds; I'd like to shout at those who are grieving: He died for nothing, for sheer madness, for nothing … for nothing … for nothing.

As the years pass by, the rain will gradually dissolve those white spots, until they disappear. But there are others that can't be erased. Engraved in our hearts are vestiges that will not fade. And every time I pass by the War Academy, with its brown granite and white spots, I say silently: Promise yourself. Take a vow. Take action. Get to work. Tell people. Liberate them from this national delusion, you, with your modest strengths. You owe it to the dead. Those white spots are screaming. Can you hear them?

They're shouting, "No more war!"

Tucholsky in his World War I German army uniform in 1915.

Berlin Business

Ignaz Wrobel, Berliner Tageblatt, January 27, 1920

Berlin business deals go something like this:

One day, there's a male voice on the phone. "Yes—hello? Yes, this is the International Union-Central—we need to speak to you as soon as possible—as soon as possible! When can we expect you?" You say they can expect you as soon as possible. Good. And then you go there.

You're received, with every sign of charm, by an extraordinarily friendly fat man. He says he's already heard a great deal about you, he's excited to meet you in person ... would you care to take a seat? A cigar? What? Oh, yes, to the point. It's about something totally new. About something absolutely and completely new, and they thought of you first—because it would never work without you, and because you're the just the perfect one for it ... What they want is—but this is still a secret—they want to start a new magazine. Oh, for God's sake! But you don't fall off your chair; instead, you look at the small fat man, well mannered in a business way, like you, with a friendly smile. Yes, he says, a new magazine—and all the top people are going to join in, and you, as a cartoonist, you should too. Now! Immediately! There are just a few little procedures, a couple of tiny formalities ... technicalities, get it? By the way, it's rather urgent. Could you provide something by tomorrow? Or the day before yesterday? You'll have to deliver right away—immediately. You bow elegantly and promise: Immediately. Good. Chairs pushed back. Handshake. My pleasure. Done.

Done.

Now you don't hear anything from the International Union-Central for four long weeks. You sat down the very next morning and sketched the most beautiful girl's leg from among your models, and you painted the greenest forest, and the bluest canopy over the bed—and you packed up the whole lot and sent it off to the I.U.C. (That has a nice ring to it! So well-funded!) And then it's done.

You don't hear anything for four weeks. Then you write a timid letter.

Nothing. Over. Poof. Then you write another letter, somewhat less timid. And still nothing. You call. A young girl's voice quacks at you and, after you tell her your long story, she says what every Berliner says on the phone, in accordance with some inexplicable law of nature: "One moment, please!"—and evaporates. Meanwhile, the switchboard cuts you off and connects you with the midwive's facility in Neukölln. Finally, you've had enough, and you go there. To the I.U.C. The small fat man receives you, he's delighted. You're not, but he is. But please! And would you like a cigar? No, you wouldn't like a cigar. You'd like some information—information about what happened to your pictures ... and to the magazine ... Ah, your pictures. And the small fat man pulls them from a pile of dusty files, your beautiful pictures with the charming canopy bed and the pretty model's leg, and says, "Yes, very nice! Exactly what we expected from you! You know, I'll have to talk to my associate about it—there are still a few snags—we have so much to do these days—just my associate ... !"

Associates run wild in Berlin. 'Sociates are like some dangerous Negro tribe. You only ever meet one of them. The other one is always the stronger one and the heart and soul of the slick operation. The one always influences the other. Yours. Associates are what make the clock tick. The buck stops with them.

Meanwhile, much oily water has flowed down the Landwehr Canal.* The weeks pass by. You've already completely forgotten the business about your pictures. One day you return to the I.U.C. Mostly out of curiosity, really. Smiling wisely and infinitely detached. Far beyond the passion of youth, you climb the carpeted stairs. And the small fat man receives you, beaming.

What happened to the magazine? Oh, they gave up on that a while ago. "You know, the current economy for magazines is ... what?" No, they want to do something entirely different. Something huge. Something really, hugely huge. A centralized milk supply facility! You grab your cap in resignation and leave, crying bitter tears.

---

* The Landwehr Canal is the main Berlin shipping route. It connects the upper and lower parts of the Spree River.

You wonder, what kind of town is this? Everyone's running around, full of big projects and planning big things. There are no theater people who aren't just about to—but it's still a secret—construct some big, new theater; there are no film jockeys not lining up some gigantic consortium; there's no publisher who isn't just about to show people what's what …

And in the meantime, nothing at all gets done.

Berlin business doesn't happen because of the entrepreneurs, but in spite of them.

Aren't there just too many projects in this blessed city? Isn't it all a little bit too much? Premature praise? Promise for the future? How come—?

Isn't everyone—in the theater, newspapers, and cinema—squandering everyone else's strengths, the talents of young artists? Older folks wouldn't put up with it—but what if you have to? When you need the money? They pump you up with hope, and you deliver designs … What hopes they are, what designs! On the day after tomorrow, they'll have forgotten everything: your project, the artist, and the sketches. And then they eagerly throw themselves into the next thing …"

"They have no remembrance. They boast and chatter and pretend that they are a great people about to do great affairs in the jungle, but the falling of a nut turns their minds to laughter and all is forgotten." That's what Kipling wrote. About apes.[*]

But wait! Is that the telephone? "This is the General Cooperative Association. Could you please … ?"

And the wise man smiles at the receiver and listens in silence, not believing a single word. And thinks of Don Quixote, a knight from Spain, who wanted to do many heroic deeds.

---

[*]   Rudyard Kipling, *The Jungle Book*.

In the Provinces

Ignaz Wrobel, Freiheit, May 16, 1920

I just returned from a short trip to the German provinces. Are you familiar with the German provinces?

Provincial Germany, where it's most dense, lives for its disdain of Berlin and for its secret admiration. It curses Berlin, when it's about politics—and it craves Berlin, when it's about the Berlin for which we Berliners don't care much: the part that's between ten and twelve o'clock at night.

Revolution, or at least what Germans call revolution, doesn't apply to the provinces. It doesn't apply to Middle Germany almost anywhere the workers don't have the upper hand politically. Something else rules there.

The bourgeoisie rules there, in its most sinister form. The old-style officer rules there. The official of the old regime rules there. And how they rule!

There have been no fresh insights there. No winds of change are blowing in. Everything is the way it's always been. There the war was lost because the traitorous homeland stabbed the noble soldiers in the back—as if the men at the front were not Germans, the homeland's own sons!—there black-white-and-red flags are still blowing in the wind; there Wilhelm the Second still rules—and his spirit, if he ever had one.

It's both amusing and sad to observe it not sinking in to their brains: Revolution? Overthrow? Change? Development? Oh, yes, they're liberal—today they call it "democratic"—they're liberal like they were liberal before and wish—indeed, with measure and determination—for gradual change ... but only as long as it doesn't hit them in the wallet. Once in a while, over a beer, in particularly progressively minded circles, they'll call the worker a good man. But only in certain circles. (The regulars at the local pub are usually the bloodthirstiest around—and any educated Bolshevist would blush

to hear how innocently the regulars would like to line up Scheidemann and Crispien and Däumig and Ebert "against the wall.")*
It all boils down to business as usual.

That's what's so peculiar about this country—Heine knew it too, back when he said that the brain power here put even God Almighty in the shade, but in reality it's the sergeant with his lash who rules—that's the peculiar thing, that all of these problems and theories and everything else we rack our brains about are ignored in practice by the blatantly couldn't-care-less attitude of the idiots who stayed. What it all boils down to is that rulers almost everywhere, due to background, education, and family tradition, can't help but see class distinctions.

And it has become such a part of their being that none of them—judges and administrators and local officials ... everyone—none of them are conscious of the fact that they instinctively operate a double standard. The whole countryside is crying bloody murder because craftsmen and even workers have been placed in administrative positions because of their views. But where else are we supposed to get them? Didn't an antiquated system shut out those others—because of their political views—from any possibility of pursuing education and skills, for centuries? You couldn't be a district administrator if Papa ran a public shop, or if you were a Democrat or a Social Democrat. They prevented it. And they wonder now why there aren't any pro-Republic or pro-democracy adminstrative officials.

They stick together like glue. They don't read anything except their own papers, which print what the reader wants and withhold the rest. (Just as any German generally reads only his party's paper, unfortunately. He should read several, in order to gain a more general perspective.) Those form an iron wall—which is nowhere more solid than in the countryside. Berlin certainly has its disadvantages, serious disadvantages—but politically speaking, it's

---

* These all were prominent Socialists and Social Democrats of the Weimar Republic, despised by right-wingers: Arthur Crispien and Ernst Friedrich Däumig were left-wing journalists and parliamentarians in the Reichstag; Philipp Scheidemann proclaimed the Republic on November 9, 1918, from the balcony of the Reichstag, and Friedrich Ebert was president from 1919 to 1925. Heinrich Heine was a German-Jewish poet and satirist who emigrated to Paris.

paradise, compared with any small German town with no industry, where the clock is still striking 1890—and won't move forward.

Only someone familiar with the immensely difficult situation of our party comrades in the provinces has any opinion about it. The workers can be enlightened—because they sense, albeit vaguely, that that's where their salvation lies. But how difficult it is for them to assert themselves against the rest! How difficult it is to achieve anything in the face of the countless, nameless harrassments of German administrative officials! (And that's something German administrative officials are good at: bullying! In that regard, they're incorruptible.) Class shenanigans are blossoming all over in those small towns. Women hold their husband's titles—though even among hens only the rooster puffs up his comb and calls "cockadoodle-doo" from the manure pile. The oversupernumerary towers over the undersuper-numerary, and every little group has its own special professional honor, and they all have their extra little privileges, that no one can take from them, and everyone is really something special—and below them all stands the worker.

Hence the enormous loathing of Berlin. Berlin means, in some respects, that everyone is equal. Berlin means that income doesn't determine one's value, nor birth the capacity of one's character. Berlin represents the Twilight of the Superiors.* They hate Berlin.

And they do their best to obstruct things. In big ways and in little ways. They sabotage the laws of the Republic whenever they can—none of that applies to them. There are still portraits of the Kaiser hanging in a large office in Hannover; it's impossible to get rid of them. Is it really impossible? I could have removed them all in one morning. And those who have the pleasure of going to Rathenow will see Hussar cavalry officers running around in their peacetime uniforms, which is fantastic—they stand there with their polished boots on the grounds of given facts—they're used to slippery parquet flooring, from life at court—and they drive their old staff cars and enjoy all of their old privileges ... None of it applies to them. There was no learning from the war here, no revolution. And if there had been? Simply deny it.

---

* A satirical reference to Wagner's opera *Twilight of the Gods* (and also Friedrich Nietsche's book *Twilight of the Idol's*)

Because in small towns, where anyone not conservative is accused of being a Bolshevist—there's work to be done. Tireless work, day in, day out. Honor and recognition to any party comrade who does what he can. His efforts are not carried out in the public eye of greater Berlin—he doesn't make a big name for himself or enjoy fame. But his efforts are valuable for all of us—useful and essential. These party comrades should be supported. They work hard. Beneath the surface.

The sun does not shine in these towns. The bourgeois order stands firm in these towns, united against progress.

Order ... ? Can you call it order when the system runs the state into the ground in four years, something not even the worst poster-Bolsheviks could ever have accomplished? When the system produces millions of dead in four years and millions of cripples, though not without first "training" their bodies and souls before their injury? Order ... ?

Berlin has a big task ahead. The provinces have an even bigger one. Because in the end, that's where the masses are. There it's enlightenment. There it's telling the truth about the war and the nation and about all of those somewhat tricky things a decent official doesn't talk about.

I'm not afraid for Berlin—no matter how much remains to be done there. But we owe our gratitude and our help to the missionaries out there in the darker regions—out there in the provinces.

150 Kaiserallee

Peter Panter, Berliner Tageblatt, June 15, 1920

You're looking for an apartment? I just happen to know of one that's vacant—please, I do a little moonlighting in that area now and then—yes, I know of one. It's in a good location—well, not right in the middle of the city—people are lucky to get one at all. . . But not too far out, either. It—the building with the vacant apartment—is on the border between Wilmersdorf and Friedenau. On Kaiserallee. 150 Kaiserallee.

You can see the building on the way from Kaiserplatz, when you go under the railway overpass—you can see it from a distance. It's a big, yellow box—I don't want to make it sound better than it is. It's really cute and simple and isn't even plastered. They say that's how the people in England are building them. But English people don't have any taste. Please, no stucco! No, I prefer our high-society buildings in western Berlin. There you know who you're dealing with.

So the building is pretty simple, with a couple of tall trees in front of it, but not so you can't see out the windows or so the rooms are dark or anything. I wouldn't recommend anything like that. You go in—that's right: it's the apartment that's vacant now, on the second floor, right-hand side. This is the fifteenth time it's been vacant, and I'll tell you why. But first you probably want to hear what kind of building you'd be moving into—you don't know me ... But you should, me and my good reputation in real estate. So, the building.

The porter lives on the ground floor, left side. The landlord put him in that little apartment instead of the musty one in the cellar. The man is a bookbinder and fiddles in his workshop all day and watches the door. You can go there and ask him about the other inhabitants. I already told him you're coming; he'll be happy to tell you. (And his apartment doesn't smell like lunch.)

Across from him, on the ground floor, right side, there's a retired senior administrative official, he says. A very progressive man, I hear.

Back in the Kapp Putsch days, he didn't go along with it and took down the black-white-and-red flag that some street urchin had stuck in his window. No, he doesn't have any kids. He lives alone with his wife. They do a lot of charity.

On the second floor there's an estate owner. That's his apartment in the city. He doesn't get deliveries from his estate in the countryside— no, here in the city he just gets the food that's on his war ration cards.

The director of a theater in Berlin lives on the other side of the second floor. He's always giving free tickets to the people in the building, is always available to his actors, and assigns roles fair and square—according to his actors.

The porter doesn't know anything else. But I can be of service. If you move in and don't waive the little four-percent commission— no, you don't want to do that, do you?

So, on the third floor there was a publisher of a—well—from a not-so-honest weekly news magazine. You can imagine, nudity and such … (But don't worry! There isn't anything like that in the apartment!) And he realized one day that he couldn't go on like that, and that it basically wasn't right to publish stuff like that—and he quit and now lives in a little fourteen-room cottage on a lake … He didn't really fit in there in the apartment building.

So that would be your vacant apartment. A nice, quiet, five-room apartment with private bath and central heating … Yes, it works. No, not now, of course. But in the winter—I'll tell you about that when I get to the landlord. The doors close tightly; the walls are so thick you can't hear what people are saying from one room to the next; the plumbing works, and there's a full-sized bathtub. And that's the apartment.

The landlord lives on the fourth floor. Yes, he lives in the building, too. He's a Berliner landlord, or more like a Friedenauer landlord, but he still hasn't raised the rent any higher than permitted by general regulations. No one has turned him in to the rent arbitration office yet. It really isn't necessary. The man voluntarily takes care of all necessary repairs, without any fuss, complaint, or ordeal. He heats the building like it's peacetime. He goes around the building every quarter-year, visiting the renters and asking them if they're satisfied or need anything …

The house at Kaiserallee, today 79 Bundesallee, where Tucholsky lived for a few years after World War I. A plaque commemorates the writer and includes the inscription, Sprache ist eine Waffe, haltet sie scharf, *Speech is a weapon, keep it sharp.*

On the fifth floor, left side, there's a young widow (in a furnished apartment). She doesn't want to remarry. She's happy on her own. On the right side of the fifth floor, there's a young woman, a single young woman. She's been living there for two years, but—according to the porter—she's never had any gentlemen visitors. And when she goes out at night, she's back by twelve at the latest, alone. That's what kind of building it is.

Those are the renters. Wait! I forgot to mention that the estate owner gave up four of the ten rooms in his double apartment to a philosophy professor who had nowhere else to live. That man hasn't applied his philosophy even once since 1914, to prove that the war ... But that's another story.

That's what kind of building it is. No, no one plays any music. The landlord's wife practices a lot, but she had a silent keyboard made, out of consideration for the renters. And the few children who live there are well behaved and play elsewhere. Babies don't cry. Plates don't rattle. Rugs are beaten only on Fridays and Saturdays— the only one who works is a balcony cleaner. Parrots don't screech. Maids don't chatter. That's what kind of building it is.

You've been listening patiently—so I'd like to be honest. I own the second mortgage on the building (there are only two), which means I'm a little interested in renting the apartment soon. Would you like ... ?

So, the best way to get there is to take the 66 or the F ...

But now you'll laugh and say something—clever man that you are—something that's unfortunately true:

"This building doesn't exist!"

Lion on the Loose!

Peter Panter, Berliner Tageblatt, July 7, 1920

On July sixth of this year, the lion, Franz King-of-the-Jungle, decided not to play along anymore in the the big predators' house in the Berlin Zoo. He broke out.

He accomplished this on the occasion of the cleaning of his cage by Chief Zookeeper Pfleiderer, when he was chased into the cage next door, by cleverly getting his tail caught in the door between the cages and thereby inhibiting its closing, waiting there for the cleaning to end, and then subjecting the clueless Pfleiderer to Roar No. 3, and running over him, through the cage door, into the open.

Lion on the loose!

This cry of alarm spread like wildfire through the pathways of our beloved Zoological Garden. The visitors' anxiety was indescribable. In their rush to escape, many left their beer on the tables, without paying—and long after the incident, honest Berliners lined up at the zoo restaurant to pay their bills. Strollers fell over, spilling their crying contents onto the walkways; older women, who usually hobbled around with difficulty, suddenly ran—it was a joy to behold. Lästerallee was swept practically clean, save for some frightened waiters perched on high tree branches, their long, black coattails hanging down like the plumage of some exotic magical birds. Lion on the loose!

Terrified people rushed out into the streets, announcing with deafening cries, "The lion's on the loose! And he took his apostrophe with him!"

The result was terrible.

While King-of-the-Jungle slowly and thoughtfully ate the small sausages hanging in the now-empty food stands, entire streetcars piled up on the streets outside. Ordinary people flung themselves, pushing and shoving, over gutters, dogs, babies, briefcases, and fat ladies who could go no farther. The lower ranks of the population quickly took advantage of the situation, scavenging the flotsam and jetsam of those who had fled, at rock-bottom prices and opening booming businesses on street corners. The upper strata, on the other hand, regained their composure as soon as they made it to their cars—carefully making sure no one was hanging on. The carriage drivers suddenly raised their prices to eighteen times the original—for the first time ever in Berlin, without asking the chief of police for permission. It was quite an uproar. In the midst of everything, a policeman, intractable and proud, moved like an Egyptian, directing traffic, and traffic stopped and watched how it was being directed and was very proud. Like in a baptized yeshiva.

Meanwhile the lion, King-of-the-Jungle, had finished his sausages. He called for the waiter—no one came. His tail twitching in irritation, King-of-the-Jungle ventured out into the open. The majestic animal nobly approached the zoo exit on Kurfürstendamm.

Berlin was roiling like an anthill. All the telephones were shrieking at once—but only calls to wrong numbers were put through. The only ones who didn't lose their heads were the operators, who continued to work in their usual cold-blooded manner, meaning no one at all got through. Reporters crowded the editors' offices at all of the big papers, "How am I supposed to get this into the evening edition?" editor Why-Always-Me complained. "Why didn't that damned lion escape half an hour ago?"

"We'll just issue an extra!" Publisher Mülvoss replied.

Cries of "Extra! Extra issue!" rang throughout the building. The typesetters' composing sticks clattered away, and the mighty rotary presses were hastily set in motion …

The stock market took the news of the lion's escape in stride. (Have you ever seen news that the stock market did not take in stride?) Coal and steel stable, spirits slightly higher, breweries flat, Jakob Goldschmidt always on top, Herbert Guttmann re-aportioned, hides stable.

When the terrible news broke at the Reichswehr Ministry, the investigating committee's subcommittee was holding a meeting to confirm its own indispensability. Breakfast, uh, sorry, the meeting broke up immediately. Two general staff officers and their advisors worked out a campaign against the lion, lickety-split, and requisitioned:

2 Army corps
1 press corps
24 extra-budgetary staff officer positions
1 cannon
1 armored land-cruiser

Meanwhile King-of-the-Jungle, ever majestic, strode, as his dear mother had taught him, through Kurfürstenstrasse to Lützowplatz. Streets and squares were devoid of people. He came to a huge lion statue. The real lion sniffed suspiciously. He raised his—something moved. What was that? Nothing. The lion gave in to his instincts.

He turned and bounded down Lützowstrasse, through Potsdamer Strasse, and stormed a large department store.

The lion, Franz King-of-the-Jungle, was a gourmand. He wanted to eat a nice, juicy little saleswoman for breakfast, such a fresh young ...

Good Lord, not again! His mouth watered, and long strings of drool got stuck in his mane. Purring, he lay down to wait.

Meanwhile, the authorities had been working feverishly. As fast and as well as they could, in their haste, they had established a Reichs-Department for Defense Against Lions, with a division specializing in Bavarian lions, and now it was just a matter of deciding whether the department would occupy the entire city hall or the Hotel Adlon—The German People's Party was alert, as always. Just a half hour later, bright blue posters covered every column and tree trunk:

"Fellow Citizens,
The lion's on the loose!
Whose fault is it?
The Jews!
Vote for the German People's Party!"

The city was in total chaos. No one dared set foot outside. Lion sightings were reported in every district—sixty-two in all. Eight big dogs were shot; the dogs' licenses confirmed the mistakes. At the home of the Konig family, Babette the maid dropped an entire tea set when the young master kissed her from behind. The poor girl fell to pieces, crying, "Jeezus, the lion!"

The Bindelband Berlin Theater directors searched desperately for the lion. They wanted to cast him in Shaw's *Androcles and the Lion*.

They drove through one street after another—but no lion.* Fire trucks wailed through the region—no lion. The lion had flown the coop.

But the lion wasn't really gone. He'd grown tired of waiting, gotten up, and was strolling through the streets. He pushed over a cherry cart, upset by the high price—and then he just kept on going..

So this was Berlin! This sad heap of stone boxes and streets as straight as arrows, all looking a little dirty—this was the cosmopolitan town of Berlin! The lion shook his head. The sparrows in his cage had told him all kinds of things—and evenings, right before feeding time, when a call would rise from the predators' house, and indeed, from the whole zoo: "Svoboda!" (Russian, as a matter of fact, is the animals' Esperanto, and the word means "freedom!")—all of them, most having never seen their natural homes, did not mean Africa or the Cordilleras or India, but Berlin! The crocodiles longed to go down the slide in Luna Park; the vultures longed to race to Ruhleben; and the wild boars dreamed of wallowing in the bars. Night after night after night. And this was Berlin? This was it?

King-of-the-Jungle shook his head again.

And they all closed in. The fire department on one side, the mountain platoon from the Reichswehr on the other, cinema operators and people who simply had to be at every premiere, journalists, ladies from the uppermost crust of society, and the Bindelbands … they all closed in. And a most extraordinary thing happened: Franz King-of-the-Jungle, the lion, ruler over all animals, His Majesty of Fauna ect. quietly let them lead him back to his cage in the big predators' house at the Zoological Garden.

And when the door had closed behind him and Chief Zookeeper Pfleiderer had scolded him, and after the swarm had dispersed, the disappointed lion lowered the tail he'd held gloriously high until then, lay down quietly, and said, with heartfelt conviction, "Never again!"

---

* The Bindelbands were fictional characters in a theatrical comedy by Donat and Anton Herrnfeld. T., however, uses "Bindelbands" as a nickname for Alfred and Fritz Rotter, two famously ruthless, Jewish brothers who ran the biggest Berlin theater empire with nine houses, including the Metropol. After piling up four million reichsmarks in debt, they filed for bankruptcy just two weeks before the Nazis came to power. They fled to Liechtenstein, where Alfred Rotter was killed by Liechtenstein Nazis. Fritz Rotter probably ended up in a French jail.

Prussian Heaven

Kaspar Hauser, Freie Welt, September 26, 1920

Peter (standing before a company of angels): "Chest out, right wing-man! For Heaven's sake, what's with that crazy formation again? Are you trying to take out the halos? Second angel, step back a little! Okay—okay ... Stop! For Pete's sake—stop wiggling your wings! Company, hut! Company, hut!"
(Heavenly Father enters right.)
Peter: "Attention! Right face!" (All heads snap right at once) "One Peter, two chief angels, eighty-six angels reporting for drill!"
Heavenly Father: "Morning, people."
Angels (in one syllable): "Goodmorningheavenlyfather!" (Pronounced: Woof!)
Heavenly Father: "Thank you! So. Anything new, dear Peter?"
Peter: "No, Your Excellency!"
Heavenly Father: "The folks are looking good! Are you getting your wages on time?"
The company: "Yes, Heavenly Father, Sir!"
Heavenly Father: "Dismiss them!"
Peter: "Dismissed!" (Company exits.)
Heavenly Father: "Come on up to the chancery with me, dear Peter. We'll have a look at the new recruits!"
Peter: "Yes, Sir!"
(Both depart.)
In the acquisitions chancery.
A worker (Coat torn and dirty. Battered face. Battered hands. Limping. Struggles to straighten up when he sees the Heavenly Father): "Good morning!"
Peter: "Jus' you wait'll yer asked! And stand at attention here! Got it? This ain't yer social-democratic party office. Got it? Name?"
Worker: "Pettenkofer!"
Peter: "I'm the staff sergeant. Name!"

Worker: "Pettenkofer!"

Peter: "That's 'Pettenkofer, Sir.' Stupid pig! What was that?"

Worker: "Pettenkoffer, S— ... uh, excuse me, but am I supposed to be here in heaven?"

Peter: "Shut your face when you speak to me! What brought you here?"

Worker: "I was murdered near Marburg. My body was lying on the road. Some students shot me. My death remains unpunished!"

Heavenly Father (rises up to his full stature—regulation height): "Get out of here! What do you think you're doing? Do you think this is some Communist hangout? We'll take those good Marburgers, when they get here, but not you! Out! To hell with you!"*

Worker (exits silently).

Heavenly Father (inside): "The things they come up with! Prussia is still under my Heaven, and my Heaven is still over Prussia!"

Peter: "Yes, Sir, Your Excellency!"

Worker (outside): "Really. . . just like down below, that's the way it is up there. Hell ... ? I was a soldier for four years!"

Heavenly Father (inside): "Ya know, it's a whole new deal in heaven, since that Wilhelm named me Prussia's Heavenly Father. Our über-ally on high, he's always saying. Too bad he lost the war ... . It was so nicely organized ... Didn't really lose it at all. Jus' looks like it. Peter!"

Peter: "Excellency?"

Heavenly Father: "Anyone else?"

Peter: "I'll go and see, your Excellency! (Opens a door.) Another recruit?"

A voice: "Yes, Sir!"

Peter: "Enter!"

Recruit: (Prussian lieutenant's uniform, clicks his heels at the door so hard that the whitewash flakes off the wall.)

Heavenly Father: "Peter, if you please!"

Peter: "Name?"

---

* In Mechterstedt near Marburg, fifteen workers were shot by right-wing corps students and officers in 1920 because they were suspected of being Communist revolutionaries. The murderers were acquitted, which caused a scandal.

Recruit: "Arco-Valley!"

Peter: "Occupation!"

Recruit: "National hero!"

Peter: "Last residence?"

Recruit: "Officially registered: Ottakring Penitentiary. Thereat for life, time served: one month. Current location: unknown."*

Peter: "Heavenly qualifications?"

Recruit (Raises his right hand. There's blood on it.)

Heavenly Father (interested): "Blood?"

Recruit (quite firmly): "Eisner, your Excellency!"

Heavenly Father (with satisfaction): "You don't say. Proceed, Peter!"

Peter: "Well, Lord Baron knows, though. You shouldn't ... Lord Baron should not kill ... ?"

Recruit (rattles off): "I made use of my national right to self-defense, in that I eradicated an international pest, as my conscience dictated. The gratitude of all good men is surely mine!"

Peter: "*Bon.* Hard work, Lord Baron?"

Recruit: "Shot in the back, Sir!"

Peter (glances questioningly at the Heavenly Father, who nods): "Passed!"

Recruit: "Sir, thank you, Sir!" (exits)

Heavenly Father: "Colossally decent man! And we shall not disarm, and we will keep our heavenly resident army—and our flag is black and white and red—and when I have all of those good Prussians and German soldiers up here with me, then I'll feel completely at ease!"

Peter: "Me, too, your Excellency!"

The German working class (from below): "Us too, your Excellency, us too!"

---

* Anton Graf von Arco auf Valley was a monarchist from the Oppenheim banking family. In 1919, he murdered Kurt Eisner, the prime minister of Bavaria, a Socialist of Jewish descent. Arco-Valley was convicted, but later paroled.

The Homeless

Peter Panter, Freiheit, October 2, 1920

There was an incident recently at a municipal homeless shelter in Berlin: "A crowd of juvenile and elderly asylum-seekers mobbed the place ... Security forces cleaned up ... Officials had their hands full ..."

When Dutch journalist Hermann Heijermans went undercover as a drifter years ago, sought refuge in a homeless shelter, and wrote about his experience for the *Berliner Tageblatt,*[*] a storm of tragic sympathy raged through bourgeois hearts, the kind that always starts buzzing when it's already too late. It soon subsided. Because the city administrators sent reports, and there was a huge stink, I believe, about how many towels each shelter inhabitant was issued—and then everything was well and good again, and no one gave any more thought to homeless shelters.

The ones who gather every night in that big building—if they were articles of clothing instead of people, they would have been discarded long ago. Many of them still want to work—and many don't want to anymore, because they can't. You struggle with Prussian authorities and their paragraphs for weeks, wandering around and waiting in dirty corridors and getting yelled at and sent all over the place, and all you have to show for it is 22.64 marks. What then? Then you start all over again.

The big machines run up above, churning out human slag down below. For each one living well up high, ten, twenty, maybe a hundred suffer down low. And even though it's accepted that there will always be people who fall, even under the best circumstances, and that there are such things as predisposition and bad blood and being

---

[*] The *Berliner Tageblatt* (Berlin Daily News) was a liberal German daily for which T. occasionally worked. Hermann Heijermans was a theatrical author and lournalist who lived in Berlin from 1907 to 1912.

responsible for one's own misfortune—however many are swept by the broom of necessity into the asylum each night, it's always someone else's fault.

Those people aren't just made like that. They become like that. But the bourgeoisie (which includes more than everyone thinks) sees things as being only static—they see the condition, but not the movements of life that brought it about. And are therefore incapable of preventing it.

Probably also because they're afraid they might lose something, and there's not that much room on the crowded ship. But there is, if you're lounging alone on the sun deck. While the mid-decks are teeming with hundreds.

Whatever the new municipal administration can do for the shelter—and I hope they can do a whole lot—nothing can atone for the gigantic sin that has made these people what they are.

A Children's Hell in Berlin

Ignaz Wrobel, Freie Welt, November 28, 1920

When you see an adult suffering, you can harden your heart and turn away. But when you see a child suffering and you're a more or less decent person, it rattles you. With the child, it's clear what the good Lord actually had in mind for mankind. With the child, pain and poverty have twice the effect, because in most cases the child is utterly defenseless, and because those big eyes are asking, "Why?"

Why?

Count Harry Kessler, the well-known pacifist,[*] has continued something that Albert Kohn previously did for many years, commissioned by the board of the German Insurance Fund for the Organization of Merchants, Craftsmen, and Pharmacists: he photographed proletarian apartments in Berlin, along with their inhabitants and especially their children. I was there when some of those shots were taken.

In books about American Indians, there's always some captive tied up, rolling around in some hovel on a bed of straw and rags. I must say, though: this was much worse. With such unspeakable poverty, the effect of efforts to establish something like order or even comfort amidst such utter destitution, despite all the misery, is twice as moving and twice as haunting. Of course it doesn't work. And it cannot work, because there's nothing there anymore: no clothes, no furniture, no lights, and no heat.

Not anymore ... what household goods are still visible in the pictures were from peacetime, bought back when people could

---

[*] T. wrote this story as part of an organized effort by journalists and welfare organizations to help starving children in Berlin after World War I. The story was originally printed in the monthly *Die Deutsche Nation* (The German Nation), edited by Count Harry Clément Ulrich Kessler, an Anglo-German diplomat and philantropist. Americans also sent food to Germany after both world wars, through Quaker religious organizations.

still afford those things. They're still there now, eaten away by time and mice, filthy, beaten up, and barely usable. But nothing can be thrown away.

In this environment people grow up, children come into being.

An advocate of law and order indignantly asks why those people have so many children. The children of the humblest proletariat owe their existence, as crass as it may sound, to the shortage of housing and beds, the lack of fuel for heating, and the inability of women to protect themselves from pregnancy (which is still prohibited under an outdated law). These children are alive because ... There's a bitter line from an old newspaper saleswoman, whose response to the question of why she brought ten children into the world was, "*Rich people go to the theater every evening ...*"

Children live there. We saw children, six or seven-year-old girls under three feet tall, and others who couldn't go outside at all because they were naked except for a little smock. Dietary conditions are downright grim. Children live on bread, margarine, and cabbage. One girl slept by a pile of rags on the stone floor, two yards away from a cellar door (. . .). The door would not close and left a gap as wide as my hand. In this proletarian world, it's practically unheard of for a child to sleep alone in a bed. "The moral depravity of the lower classes"—any preacher who utters something like that should be boxed on the ears with a Bible. Let them go and see for themselves: apartments not fit for a horse accustomed to the imperial stables, those dank, pitch-black basement holes with a couple of cots where children sleep—they should take a look at those!

And the worst thing about it is this: we're not talking just about the unemployed, but about families earning low wages in meager jobs. Which are useless. There was a time when factory workers were not considered members of the lumpenproletariat. But today?

Rickety, tubercular, scrofulous, and run-down children. Their mothers live for the most part on whatever's left from their children's Quaker feed. (Hey, comics! How about a little scoffing at America?) The children see everything, hear everything, and experience it all. What kind of people will they become?

This time, the bourgeois press, which doesn't usually take much notice of these things, reacted a little, seeing not the pacifist in Kessler, but the Count. To the benefit of the unfortunate. There will be a relief effort. And may every thousand-mark bill be blessed—no matter who gives it. Because this is about German children.

But at this point we must pause to remember. In light of these photos, we must consider *who* sent the German working class into this hell! *Who* wasted these people's blood and money for four years? *Whose* megalomaniacal foolhardiness turned half of Europe into a battlefield and the other half into a base with headquarters in which they spread their butter as thick as a finger and guzzled alcohol until it ran out of the gentlemen's eyes? *Who* needlessly misspent, used up, shot away, and squandered billions and billions?

Hindenburg, Ludendorff, Helfferich, & Co.[*]

Yet even without that war waged by raving-mad Prussians, these images are an indictment. Normal citizens, if they have a heart, will feel that stirring of teary-eyed compassion that moves them to say, "How terrible! How horrible!"

But not *one* of those who earn their living from the misery of the defenseless, not one of those whose broad beds perch upon the corpses of children, will allow even a penny of their capitalistic revenue to be taken away. Help! Bolshevism! And that twenty-four-year-old oaf who got married yesterday and went into Daddy's business making ready-to-wear clothing, he'll be indignant and won't understand when you tell him that *this* is what the flip side of his $120,000 annual income looks like.

These pictures indict the world. A children's hell in Berlin?

The children's hell of capitalism.

---

[*] Paul von Hindenburg and Erich Ludendorff were conservative politicians and two of the most influential military leaders during the German effort in WWI; Treasury Secretary Karl Helfferich financed the war through loans. He also fought against reparations imposed upon Germany by the Versailles treaty.

Three Generations

Peter Panter, Die Weltbühne, January 5, 1922

Speaking of Berlin prostitutes, one of the first and oldest kinds has all but disappeared. She served under Kaiser Wilhelm, an old, fat, hard worker, bursting bodices, alarming young lads—and you had to hail from faraway Wollenhagen on the Persante river to find this enormous mass of femininity appealing—eighty cents a pound. These girls sat, diluvial deposits, in pubs generally decorated in intimate old-German style, with aphorisms hanging on the walls among gilded Trumpeters of Säckingen wallpaper blowing a bluesy *God protect you ...* * The actual orchestra was playing Wagner and military marches, but they looked like slightly degenerate butchers' wives. "Whatcha got there?" They supported thrones and altars. But not a pretty sight. An oil pump.

The second generation hailed from the time of the big agricultural fairs, when the good old honest country boys, faces ruddy from the fresh air and aged red wine, came to Berlin to get some relief from the stinky stall smell, the wife, and the mortgage, to this city they hated, loathed, and loved. That was back when people felt more secure than they do now, because gold coins were jingling in their pockets (you knew exactly where and how—such a comforting feeling!). It was the time of the Metropol Theatre and court balls. This vintage of women was significantly more refined than the first—cleverer with makeup, lingerie, gentlemen, and relationships. These still traveled first-class—they drove cars. Their pubs were decked in champagne-Rococo, vacillating between everything Louis and a charming Baroque, and their ideal life resembled the second curtain at the Metropol. Their elegance was just as improbable as their lo-

---

* *Der Trompeter von Säckingen* is a nineteenth-century opera that was a favorite among petit-bourgeois theatergoers.

calities; they were so outrageously Berlinerisch[*] that foreigners could only laugh at them at first. But because they were also so naughty, the weary wanderer eagerly overlooked their lack of quality in the cultural realm. The Palais was established then. (The connoisseur would bite his tongue rather than say *palais de danse*. There was only one: the Palais.) In this second-generation era, a raucous frivolity erupted in Berlin, which seemed hectically American then, something we might consider slightly old-fashioned/Biedermeierish and almost cozy today. "My God, how harmless the people were back then!" But they weren't. They were wheeling-dealing, profit-seeking underlings. Everything went bust in 1914. Though one must admit, objectively, that a pound-countess [Goldmark] at an evening with, say, Toni Grünfeld was still better than today's ... But we'll soon see that. In any case, Victor Hollaender played music, everyone in Berlin sang Julius Freund, and by and large, love and lust were industrialized.[**] Pretty decent and honorable, compared to today. "Thank God, not everyone's the same!" A four-suit deck.

Today ... dear friends, there's no denying that there have been better times than our own ... The third generation, today's, is the palest by far. But it's not as if the prostitutes of the past linger on the lampshade of memory, thoroughly idealized ... No, no. It was only those medium-sized times, which followed the steel bath that managed to coin the phrase "john with valuable foreign currency." And for orientation, let's just parade the faces of the three generations by once more. The first were fattened Valkyries with the futile attitude of coquettish loveliness; the second often displayed tough, gamine-like traits, many wearing their hair cut short like a boy's, and this pageboy sported a narrow mouth—she knew the Sacher-softness of her men ... [***] But the third, ah, the third ...

Never have there been so many prostitutes in Berlin who really aren't. They're from the most diverse schools, snort the friendliest

---

[*] Berlinerisch is what T. calls wannabes who are pretending to be Berliners, as opposed to "Berlinisch", i.e. real Berliners (see also page 32)
[**] Victor Hollaender and Julius Freund were Berlin composers; Hollaender's son Friedrich wrote songs for Marlene Dietrich. Toni Grünfeld was an actor.
[***] A wordplay on the name of Leopold Ritter von Sacher-Masoch, a writer of erotic novels; T. implies that the clients of these prostitutes were Masochists.

things, inject their wrists till they're raw and cover them with wide bracelets—they've long since lost the stability and precision of a proper prostitute. The heart of every well-educated lady of the old regime must skip a beat, as we say, when they see this … They are often very thin; their faces are colorless and featureless—there isn't much to them, either good or bad. Eels.

And if the good old whore story began with a mawkishly sentimental seduction scene, three hundred grammophone recordings of conversations with these young ladies played at once would go something like this:

"I once had a friend, you know, a fantastic man—and then he got so mean—my bags were in Bristol—do you think he picked them up? But when the lady told me that, I says (eyebrows raised), 'Really,' I says, if you think the jewelry belongs to you, prove it!' I says, 'I'll take it up with the district attorney!' I says. You know, sometimes I'm in a pretty bad mood. But when I'm in a good mood, I could smash everything to pieces. I was so sick. I spent eight weeks in the clinic with Professor (first-rate name)—the professor said he'd never seen a constitution like mine … Got cocaine—?"

"Petals in the wind." You could call it that. You could also say, "Always a whore." For through the pompous self-assertions, through the inventive imitations of a regal tone of voice, there squeaks a pathetic little mistress you might actually pity.

Their pubs these days are expressionistic (though even that's already a bit passé); there in the insane petulance of misunderstood oil-snobbery, the bear-market man leaves his worries behind. Crazed music (which is only tolerable when it's brilliantly executed) rips through the room; among them sit these smooth things, neither woman, nor girl, nor human, nor boy. Their guys are all from Grosz, because they're successful. But that might be gone in the morning—and because the johns aren't financially sound, the women aren't either. Red today, rouge tomorrow. It's the Republic's fault, of course.

Amusements always resemble the businesses people are trying to recover from. These women and these pubs are the seamy side of international foreign currency exchange.

Berlin Love

Theobald Tiger, Die Weltbühne, October 13, 1921

If it's love you're looking to find
from Köpenick to Westend:
lower your gaze, then,
and distinguish the three basic kinds:
There are women with parted hair,
stamped silver on bosoms fake,
in reform dress or blouse of their own make,
once—long past!—most clean and fair,
(now a dunkel weiss).
Through rain and storm
they walk in wood and hall alone,
loden cap jauntily across one ear,
Only themselves or Tagore to hear …
Is this the one?
They recite feuilletons before you get them in bed.
So very noble.
But not well bred.

Then there are those with bottoms of silk,
in fur-collared coats of velvet or damask—
about her parents, you mustn't ask.
You three love both, as she's true to your ilk.
Experts call your efforts big nights on the town.
Take her to the theater, a movie!
She knows the latest dances and every pair,
and every month has freshly colored hair …
Is she the one—is she?
She doesn't say much.
But when she does it's sticky glue.
And she'll take everything from you.

Will it be one of Thalia's inclination?
She reveals when she's together with you,
what a cad her director is, true,
leading them all into temptation—
She'd never do that. (Almost never.)
A river of speech:
rehearsals, premieres, gossip too—
Master of acting and speech, so rare,
playing Olala and Iphigenia with care …
Is she the one for you?
By Papa Rickelt! Sweet at every stage:
She loves.
But buries you at an early age.

So go, wand'ring lover, house to house.
Berlin is big.
Just pick one out!'

---

*   Rabindranath Tagore was a Bengali philosopher, composer, and novelist who won the Nobel Prize for Literature in 1913. Thalia is the Greek muse of entertainment and the theatrical arts. Papa Rickelt was a folksy actor.

Mr. Wendriner Makes a Phone Call

Kaspar Hauser, Die Weltbühne, July 6, 1922

*On the afternoon when Walther Rathenau was laid to rest,
the entire Imperial Postal Service paused to observe the occasion,
from two o'clock until ten minutes past two.*

"If he won't accept the invoice, I'll just call 'im on the phone. Just
put the envelopes on that chair. Which district is Skalitzer's? Königstadt? Wait a minute … Well? Hmmm? Hey, what's going on? Operator! Why aren't you answering? Did'ya see that? She didn't say
why she's not answering. Operator! Doesn't this phone work? Miss
Tinschmann, what's wrong with the phone? Doesn't it work? How
many times have I gotta tell you …

"What? What's that? The switchboard is closed? What does that
mean? Why? Oh, yeah, 'cuzza Rathenau. Thanks, you can go now …
'Cuzza Rathenau. That's good. Very fitting, that is. The man was a
royal businessman and a great statesman. No denying it. Scandalous, that he was shot. Truly a decent man! I knew the old Rathenau
well—now those were businessmen, weren't they! Outstanding funeral at the Reichstag, wasn't it? Very impressive. Brilliant lead story
in the morning paper—excellent. Yeah, the government'll have to
resort to drastic measures—already issued a decree, they did. Out'a
the car to shoot—outrageous! The cops should …

"Operator! I guess the ten minutes aren't up yet. Must've been brilliant shots, those boys. Maybe even officers … But it's unthinkable:
Walter's buddies from the regiment were all at our place for dinner
back then—all of 'em such nice, fine people! Some swell guys among
'em! I was really glad when that boy became a reserve officer!

"Operator! Operator! These ten minutes are getting a little long,

Operator! And if you're on strike just one minute longer than ten—
I'll lodge a complaint!

"Operator! I've gotta reach that old Skalitzer! Crazy idea, shutting
off the phone! That won't bring 'im back to life. Better to divvy up
taxes fairly, that'd be more in line with the dearly departed!

"Operator! Who's gonna shut the phone down when I'm gone?
No one! Meshugge, turning off the phone! How'm I s'posed to reach
Skalitzer now? He'll prob'ly be out to lunch later! Scandalous! Better wages is what they want—that's all. What is this, turning off the
phone right under our noses, in broad daylight?! There was plenty
goin' on under the Kaiser, but I never seen nothin' like this! Outrageous! It's a public nuisance! Whether they kill each other or not—it
shouldn't get in the way of business! Besides: a Jew shouldn't cause
such a fuss over 'imself! That just 'xacerbates anti-Semitism. Since
November ninth, there just ain't been no order in this country anymore. Do they really have to cut us off from the phone? Who'll
reimburse my loss, if I don't reach Skalitzer?

"Operator! Now you just listen—they're demonstratin' outside!
Look—with red flags—it's kind'a nice! What're they singin'?

"Operator! They'll just keep it up until there's another revolution!
Operator! The whole republic can just kiss my …

"Operator! Operator! In my political opinion … Operator! Finally! Operator! Gimme Königstadt!"*

---

* Herr Wendriner is a recurring character in T.'s writing, a bourgeois Jewish
businessman, then one of many in Berlin. T. was sometimes criticized for having created an anti-Semitic stereotype with the Wendriner character, something
he always refuted. Walter Rathenau was a liberal politician and the first Jewish
secretary of state in Weimar Germany. He was shot and killed in 1922 by three
anti-Semitic right-wingers who where part of a secret terrorist organization con-
nected to the Reichswehr, the German army.

The Family

Peter Panter, Die Weltbühne, January 12, 1923

The Greeks, who knew so well what friendship was, described their relatives with a term that is the superlative of the word "friend." I still don't understand this.

—Friedrich Nietzsche

On the sixth day of creation, when God saw what he had made, everything was good, but the family wasn't there yet, either. He would pay for his premature optimism, and humankind's longing for paradise can be understood primarily as the burning desire to be allowed, just once, to live in peace without a family. What is a family?

The family (*Familia domestica communis*, the Common House Family) runs rampant in Middle Europe and usually stays that way. It consists of a collection of many people of various genders whose main objective is to stick their noses in your affairs. When a family achieves larger proportions, we call them "relatives" (see dictionary under "M"*). The family usually appears concentrated in dreadful clumps, and would be in constant danger of being shot during rebellions because it absolutely will not come apart. Generally speaking, the family vehemently loathes itself. Membership in the family conveys a germ that is widely distributed: every member of the guild is constantly taking offense. That old lady sitting on the famous couch is an historic forgery: first of all, a lady never sits alone, and second, she's always taking offense—not just on the couch, but sitting, standing, lying, and on the subway.

The family knows everything about each other: when Karl had the measles, whether Inge is happy with her tailor, when Erna is going to marry the electrician, and that Jenny will stay with her husband for good, after their last fight. News such as this spreads between the

---

* M for mishpocha, Yiddish for family.

hours of eleven a.m. and one p.m., through the defenseless telephone. The family knows everything, but disapproves of it on principle. Other wild Indian tribes either live with daggers drawn or smoking a peace pipe: the family can do both simultaneously.

The family is rather exclusive. It knows what the youngest nephew does in his spare time, but woe to the young man who gets it in his mind to marry a stranger! Twenty opera glasses are fixed upon the poor victim, forty eyes squint skeptically, and twenty noses sniff suspiciously: "Who is it? Is she worthy of that honor?" It's the same on the other side. In these cases, both parties are usually convinced that they've sunk way below their level.

But once the family takes the strangeling into its lap, the clan lays its big hand on this brow, too. Even the new member must sacrifice at the altar of relations; there is no holiday that does not belong to the family! Everyone curses; no one likes to—but Lord have mercy, when someone's missing! Heaving a sigh, everything bends under the bitter yoke …

The family's "social get-together," though, usually ends in a fight. That certain sweet-sour tone is prevalent in its manners, which can best be compared with the mood right after a summer afternoon storm. But that doesn't impede the cozy ambience. The blessed Herrnfelds once put a scene in one of their plays in which a dreadfully divided family celebrated a wedding ceremony, and after everyone had bashed in everyone else's head, a prominent family member stood up and said in the sweetest tone in the world, "And now we come to the drinking song!" They always come to the drinking song.

Even back in Georg Simmel's* great sociology, we read that no one hurts anyone else as much as a close member of the caste, because he knows exactly where the victim's most sensitive spots are. They know each other too well to love each other dearly, and not well enough to like each other.

They are very close to each other. A stranger would never dare to get as close to your body as your sister-in-law's cousin, on account

---

* Donat and Anton Herrnfeld were theater producers in pre-WWI Berlin. Georg Simmel was a sociologist who influenced the Frankfurt School and the Chicago School. His most important work was *The Philosophy of Money.*

of the relations. Did the ancient Greeks call their relatives "most beloved"? The younger generation today calls them something else. And suffers from the family. And later establishes its own and becomes exactly that.

No family member ever takes another family member seriously. If Goethe had had an old aunt, she would surely have gone to Weimar to see what the boy was up to, would have taken a mint *cachou* from her *pompadour*, and eventually would have left again, thoroughly offended. Goethe, however, did not have an aunt like that, but he did have peace instead—and that's how *Faust* came to be. The aunt would have found it excessive.

On birthdays, it is advisable to give gifts to the family. There isn't much point, though—they usually exchange everything.

It is utterly impossible to withdraw from the family. In fact, my old friend Theobald Tiger sings:

Never start anything with the relatives—
For that will go awry,
for that will go awry!

But these lines came from stupendous ignorance. One doesn't start anything with the relatives—the relatives see to it themselves.

And when the whole world comes to an end, you're afraid that a graceful angel will come to you in the great beyond, gently waving his palm branch, and saying, "Hey, aren't we related somehow?" And hastily, alarmed and thoroughly heartbroken, you flee. To hell.

But it doesn't do you any good. Because they're all sitting down there, all the rest of them.

Mornings at Eight

Ignaz Wrobel, Die Weltbühne, June 28, 1923

I saw a dog the other day—he was going to work. He looked kind of like an overstuffed sofa bolster decorated with furry tassels, and he wagged his way down Leipziger Strasse in Berlin; he was completely serious, looking neither to the left nor the right, not sniffing anything, and not doing anything else at all. He was most definitely going to work.

And why shouldn't he have been doing that? Everyone around him was doing it.

A stream of going-to-workers was rushing through the city. Just as they did every morning. They trotted to work, that most sacred place of Germans. The dog didn't actually have any reason to be there—but since he was going to work too, he was welcome.

Two serious men sat in the trolley—smoking, clean-shaven, with full stomachs, and completely content—and looked out the window. At moments like this, you wish for a miracle, for balloons to sprout from the helmet of the policeman on the corner, for example, so their faces might register some surprise, just this once! The trolley passed a tennis court. The golden sun shone on the light yellow surface—the weather was glorious, much too nice for Berlin. And one of the serious men grumbled, "They've got nothing to do—look at them! Playing tennis at eight in the morning! They should be going to work!"

Yes, they should. Because that's why man is here in this world, to do earnest work, the kind that fulfills the whole man. Does it have purpose? Is it harmful or useful? Does it bring pleasure? ("You tellin' me work is fun? You're effin' crazy!") None of that matters. It just has to be work. And you should go there in the morning. Or else there's no point to life.

And when everything grinds to a halt, because the railway workers are on strike or it's a holiday, they all sit around and don't know what to do. Nothing's going on inside them, or outside them either, so what's the point? There is no point ...

And then they run around like schoolkids who've been given a free hour by mistake—they can't go home, and they're not in the mood to have fun ... They snooze and wait. For the next work day. That's one reason, among others, why the German revolution failed; they didn't have time to revolt, because they were going to work.

And it should also be mentioned that a person can snooze while doing sports, which these days happens like a card game: according to the rules and exquisitely monotonous. But in the end, it's always better to train than to monkey around in a black robe ... [*]

Yes, they go to work. "What kind of work do you do?"—"None, Sir; it does us."

The dog did not jump. People don't hop in the streets. The street serves to—we know that already. And the tempting, low-hanging, patriotic poster ... the dog paid no attention to it.

He went to work.

---

[*] A reference to T.'s dislike of the (mostly conservative) German judges and district attorneys who used to wear black robes.

To Do! To Do!

Theobald Tiger, Die Weltbühne, July 10, 1924

In the newspaper today, I read:
Los Angeles has a schnapps society,
and people are afraid it will spread
throughout the land—that reminded me:
I really should write to Edith again.
Her letter from California here
since January, I've shunned the pen,
procrastinated now half a year.
It's wrong. It leaves me no peace, it's true.
But … I have ever so much to do.

My doctor tells me to exercise;
there's some kind of school for sports …
And up in the attic so much old stuff lies
that I really should take to the poor!
To Father's grave, have I had a look?
I mean to, but it always eludes me.
I've wanted to read the yellow book,
along with Simmel's sociology.
How often I've yearned to see Friedrichsruh!
But … I have ever so much to do.

One day, when the trumpets begin to blow,
the Berliner will rise up from his grave.
He'll stand before all, in the front row—
("So important, all those contacts I made!")
God, our Lord, ever so peaceful and mild,
walking over water, will ask, indeed,
"What did you do in this world, my child?
Berliner! What kind of life did you lead?"
The Berliner will say, rather vaguely, too:
"None at all … I had too much to do."

Kurt Tucholsky

Evenings after Six

Peter Panter, Vossische Zeitung, *September 27, 1924*

Blessed is he who walks apart,
Though no hate he bears,
Holds a friend within his heart;
And with him he shares.
What men cannot know
Or do not care for,
Through the labyrinth of the heart
Wanders in the night.

—Unknown poet[*]

After six o'clock in the evening, all kinds of people take walks in Berlin's Tiergarten park, arms linked and hands clasped—and they're all right. It's like this:

He picks her up from work, or she him. The two of them stretch their legs a little; after sitting in the office all day, the evening air does them good. Along the gray streets, through the Brandenburg Gate, for example—and then through the Tiergarten. What do they do along the way? They talk about their day. And what happened that day? Anger.

While our language claims that we "swallow our anger," that simply isn't true. We don't swallow anything. At the time, you can't answer—the boss, the colleague, the doorman—it's not advisable; the other guy gets more money, so he's right. But it all comes back, after six o'clock in the evening.

The loving couple wanders through the Tiergarten's leafy green

---

* These lines are from Johann Wolfgang von Goethe's poem *An den Mond* (To the Moon), so T. is being ironic. English translation by Margarete Muensterberg, *A Harvest of German Verse,* 1916.

corridors, and he tells her what happened at work. First the report. Maybe you've already noticed how battle reports after such clashes usually go: the reporter is the epitome of peaceful goodwill, and it's the evil enemy who's the Indian gone stark raving mad. It goes something like this: "I sez, Mr. Winkler, sez I, Filing it like that just won't work." (In the most peaceful tone in the world—gentle, mild, and wise.) "He sez, Do you mind! Sez he, I'll file it any way I like!" (brisk, brusque, and extremely irritated).

Then the Supreme Commander again: "I sez, totally calm, I sez, Mr. Winkler, but we can't file it like that, because then the C mail will get mixed up with the D mail! And he starts shouting. I had no right to order him around, and he won't do anything that anyone else tells him to do. Howdaya like that?" When in reality, of course, both raised a raucous ruckus. But sometimes it was the boss, and you really can't talk back to him. And so you "swallow it," and now you're unloading it. "Howdaya like that?"

Lotte thinks it's scandalous. "Hah! Well, whaddaya know?" That feels good, a soothing salve for an injured heart—finally you can get it all out! "I really wanted to tell him: Do it all yourself then, if you don't like it! Why do I have to put up with such a stupid man! The guy doesn't understand a thing, I tell you! He's clueless! The way he's doing it now, of course his C mail will get mixed up with his D mail—dead certain! Well, I don't care. At least I know what to do: I'll just let him do it. He'll see how far he gets that way!" A shy expression of admiration touches our knight on horseback. He's right.

But she has something to report, too. "What that Elli is up to, you can't even imagine! Miss Friedland had a new blouse on yesterday, and she said on the phone—we all heard it: You know where some of the girls at the office get money for new blouses! Whaddaya think? And Elli doesn't have a fiancé anymore! Hers left a long time ago—went to Bromberg!" Bam, the whole line fighting with the third floor—all-out war. "I didn't say a thing ... but I thought to myself, Well, I thought, where'd you get your silk stockings? We all know! She gets picked up every other evening, ya know, always has the car wait down the next block ... but we figured it out right away! Outrageous, that's what she is!" He grasps her arm and says, "You don't say!" And now she's right.

And so they stroll. All of them, the many, many pairs of lovers in the Tiergarten, they talk to each other, they tell each other their troubles, and then they're all right. They restore balance to life once again. It just wouldn't be healthy, going home like that, with all that angry opposition from the last nine hours bottled up inside. It must come out. Incorrect balances, stupid telephone conversations, missed replies, suppressed rudeness—it all works its way out, into the open—one big orgiastic celebration of workday hindsight. The blue veil of twilight sinks into the trees and bushes, and the loving couples walk arm in arm along the paths, killing bosses, destroying the competition, stabbing enemies right in their false hearts. The audience is grateful, attentive, and infinitely trusting, applauding without pause and calling out, "Again!" at the best moments. It kills, destroys, and stabs right along. It is ally, friend, brother, and spectator, all at once. It's so nice to perform for it.

After six o'clock in the evening, work is reorganized, employees promoted, bosses demoted, and, above all, salaries set. Who would change rates? Who would allocate bonuses fairly? Grant vacation with extra pay? The lovers, after six o'clock in the evening.

The next day, it starts all over again. You go to work, nice and relaxed, yesterday's agitation shaken off, gone; your coat and hat are hanging in the closet, the books straightened up on the shelf—all right then! Let the troubles begin! There it is, right at three o'clock—the same story as yesterday: Mr. Winkler doesn't want to sort the mail; Miss Friedland wrinkles her nose; the vacation list has a hole in it; and there's no bonus in sight. Anger, stubbornness, harsh conversations on the phone, muffled silence in the office. There's a flash of yellow lightning. Thunder rumbles. The refreshing rain won't come until evening, with her, with him, arm in arm in the Tiergarten.

Where there's peace on earth and everything's fine with the couples, the defendant has the last word—and they're all, every one of them, right.

Ape Cage

Peter Panter, Die Weltbühne, October 16, 1924

The Ape (on the subject of the visitors): "How nice that they're all behind bars!"

—Old Simplicissimus

A troop of baboons from Abyssina lives in a cage in the Berlin Zoo, and the public makes a fool of itself in front of them daily, from nine to six. *Hamadryas hamadryas* l., sitting still in its cage must think humans are a childish and idiotic species. These are Old World apes, they have rump calluses and cheek pouches. The cheek pouches are not visible. The rump calluses turn a flaming red, as if each ape were seated on a brick of Edam cheese. The troop lives in a giant cage, visible from three sides; from one side, you can see through to the other side: bars, the apes, bars again, and the zoo visitors beyond. There they stand. Papa, Mama, the little one; well rested, after their nice Sunday morning baths, with clean nostrils. They are easily amused, equipped with a blend of curiosity, rational superiority, and a dose of good-natured mockery. Morning theater—the apes are supposed to perform for them. A very specific act.

At first, it's quiet in the ape cage. The animals sit on the upper shelves, singly, in pairs, and in threes. There's a married pair sitting way up high—two animals totally focused on each other, hugging each other, each listening to the other's heartbeat. Several are picking lice off each other. The ones being deloused have a look of contentment on their faces, surprisingly similar to that of shaving-creamed men at barber shops; they look dignified and are in complete agreement with the good work being done. The delousers search, softly and steadily, carefully combing the hair back, probing, and sometimes sticking what they find into their mouths … One crouches on the floor, caveman at the fire, long arms shoveling bits of nut into its mouth. One approaches the bars in front and sits down in front of the audience, a look of contentment on his face, as if he's at the theater, settling into a comfortable position … So, let it begin.

It begins. Mrs. Dembitzer appears, firmly convinced that the ape has been waiting there since seven that morning to watch her say, "Tse, tse, tse," to him. The ape watches her … with a divine expression. Mrs. Dembitzer is infinitely superior. So is the ape. Mr. Dembitzer throws some bread crust at the ape's nose. The ape picks it up, sniffs it, and slowly puts it into his mouth. His heavily creased peasant mouth begins to move. Then he calmly looks around. The Dembitzer child tries to tease the ape with a stick. Suddenly the ape is six thousand years old.

Something must be happening over there. There's a lusty, furtive expression in the observers' eyes, which grow small and wink. The women vacillate from disgust to dread to a feeling: *nostra res agitur* [this is about us]. What is it? The apes on the other side have become the subject of a stimulating visual inspection. They're playing something, and it's not Mah-Jongg. The audience is indignant, entertained, excited, and pleasantly amused. A quiet wave of guilty conscience ripples through the crowd—everyone feels it. "Mama!" a child says loudly, "What's that red cord that ape has?" Mama doesn't say. My dear child, it's the red thread running through the entire history of the world.

The apes have begun to move. The scene is rather like a coed bath in Zinnowitz. Walking around, touching, poking each other, feeling each others' organs, along with their own … Two little ones run around in circles, screeching. A bearded consistorial councilor talks earnestly with a teacher about these difficult times. An abandoned female ape keenly follows the activity of her ex. A young ape talks with his publisher—the publisher vigorously waves his arms and legs and takes another fifty percent. Two united Social Democrats have become rational and pragmatic; they watch the young ones, disapproving—they're about to reach a compromise. Two apes are discussing a secret known only to them. The audience is slightly disappointed, because there's not much indecent activity. The apes are not disappointed by the audience at all—they don't really expect any more. If we had a revue stage instead of those boring sports arenas full of pilfered pranks—what a revue scene it would be!

Apes from Gibraltar used to live in the huge cage. Large, dark, hairy fellows, larger than humans, with huge, ancient Negro faces. One mother had a baby—she always held it to her breast, a black Madonna. They all died. Apparently, the climate wasn't good for them. They're not the only ones who can't tolerate this climate.

Do the apes have a president? A Reichswehr? And high courts of appeal? Maybe they had all of those things in distant Gibraltar. And now they're dead, because someone took it all away from them. Because real apes can't live without them.

The entrance to the Berlin Zoo with the Elephant's Gate;
one of the few places that still looks like it did in the 1920s.

Berlin's Best

Peter Panter, Die Weltbühne, *January 20, 1925*

He's up on the wall over there, he gave me that picture himself, and he wrote something on the back. The face with the gray mason's stubble is looking past Mr. Courteline. ("We can't understand each other," the painting says, "but we get along. Maybe that's why.")

The Frenchman asks, "Who's that?"

"Heinrich Zille," I reply. "*C'est un peintre allemande.*" But that's not true. He's much more than a German painter.

His greatest book is out now, the one about Berlin: *Berlin Stories and Pictures* (published by Carl Reissner in Dresden, 1924).

Paris has, among the living incarnations of its municipal sense of humor, a man who sometimes comes close to Zille as an artist: Poulbot, the children's Poulbot, who illustrated the cheeky, impudent, cobblestone-hopping, precocious, and sympathetic *gosse.*[*] On Christmas Eve last year, he even presented his *gosses* with gifts. Vienna has those who trivialize its municipal sense of humor, who can entirely ruin one's own sense of humor. Berlin has both.

It's so difficult to speak of Berlin humor, because a host of petty-bourgeois scribblers are flooding the field with kitschy drivel. The kid- or yarn-gloved Right grabs the "little people" by the scruff of the neck and parades them by the pleased bourgeois public, always with that fatal attitude of supposed genuineness, with the tone of false sympathy, false dread, false humor, Lord have mercy. It's the same humor with which Supreme Court Clerk Lehmann dresses up as a pimp at the Jury-free Ball—everyone knows he isn't one, thank God, but it looks so romantic. It's the humor of the "funny pages," which presents the ready-to-wear manufacturers with the comically-dirty, comically-pregnant, comically-drunk victims of their temporary

---

[*] Francisque Poulbot was a French caricaturist for *Le Rire* and *L'Assiette au Beurre.* Georges Courteline was a French writer and a friend of Kurt Tucholsky.

masters—that makes their private bathroom on Bayreuther Strasse sparkle so nicely again. "Ugh, how funny!" Add another drop of schmaltz to the soup—Grunewald with its evening pines, my ass—then the disaster is complete, and it turns your stomach to see Berlin discredited like that.

Before and during the war, Heinrich Zille sometimes fell victim to such employers. He had to draw things that were required of him and that someone else would have drawn worse; he came out with a frankly horrible series during the war, which was equally distant from Berlin and the war, and the only thing it had in common with them was that it offered both up for sale. Sometimes he had to joke when he really wanted to do something entirely different. Of the drawings in this wonderful book, not even one-thirtieth were published before. All the papers praise it, but none would dare to print anything reflecting even a glimmer of their splendor. Why not? It's simple, really. A book doesn't have any ads.

*

Heinrich Zille's secret lies in the first sentence of the autobiography that introduces his book: "In 1872, I trained as a lithographer." Zille is a craftsman. He learned a trade, and he learned it well, and he never abandoned that foundation of craftsmanship. It's interesting to observe all the stages in the book: from naturalistic effort "to copy the thing" through to the final formulation that no longer requires it and can confidently leave it out (but different from those young gents who scribble because they aren't capable of anything at all). Zille's soul is all Berlin: soft, big mouth, warm feet whenever possible, and "nothing's all that bad."

Family tree: petty bourgeois. "My Father" is a pretty typical piece: the old man is standing at the bench, solemnly engrossed in his work, while two "gypsies" are looking in from outside, vagabonds, laughing, with a little cheek, a little envy, and a little despair, at the petty-bourgeois castle the man has built there. Ultimately, it's this aspiration to a higher class that Zille is vetting: the petty-bourgeoise and the wannabes. (He rarely reaches beyond that; when he draws "refined folk," they're either conscious exaggerations, the way they appear in the eyes of those down below, or touching anachronisms.)

Here, among the lower middle class, is the ideal that Zille soon made known and beloved. "Restaurant under the Walnut Tree," with the little yellow lamp on the wobbly table, chubby Maria behind the counter, the busy pregnant woman with her shopping basket, and the kid, the indefatigable kid, with his shirt untucked both in front and in back, and his runny nose, not to mention the rest, who's shouting, hopping, dancing, and picking his nose. So far, so good. Zille was a funny-pages kind of guy, an infallibly safe bet, much appreciated by all respectable people as a champion of their order, which he promoted by means of skillfully depicting its opposite. That is where the real Zille begins.

There, where the proletariat becomes the lumpenproletariat; there, where it no longer pays to work—work and despair! There, where it no longer makes sense to do anything anymore, where there's nothing maternal to catch you when you fall, only the water—there he forged for himself an alarming stature. Tragedy? In Berlinese? In Berlinese: totally mum, thought-provoking, man becoming the scrap heap, though he's stopped proclaiming it.

Here Zille touches on Kollwitz. Though she's playing a symphony, while he's plunking out a tune on an old barrel organ, and we're crying our eyes out. The word of words appears in this book, irrefutable, once and for all, scarcely stylized, probably copied, simply grown out of the ground of muck, booze, tuberculosis, and tenement squalor. "Ya know, ya betta don't think too hard on it." But some do think about it; those are the dangerous ones ...

Amorality is in Zille's blood. He does not judge, he draws. He does not feel superior, he feels. Bible? Civil Code? His folk are way beyond that—to them, preachers and district judges are more or less unpleasant representatives of a system whose effect is predominantly exemplified in the amount of time it wastes. Get arrested, wait, get thrown in jail, wait again, be admonished, snarled at, convicted ... it all takes so long, but there isn't anything else.

That's Zille, our Zille. The child's corpse in the trash bin; the pregnant woman who doesn't know if the one in her arms will still be alive when the one in her belly arrives; George, whose rants the policeman no longer hears because it's not worth his while; the woman who goes into the water with two children, quickly, hurry, no will

Heinrich Zille, Berlin's foremost draftsman.

to go on, don't stop; the group of children singing "Be-e-loved ho-omeland—bye-bye—Plötzensee,"* a piece of rare tragedy. You laugh and then notice that not one of the children is undamaged. Every-thing is distorted, shortsighted, afflicted with the English disease, stunted; a living skeleton is decomposing on its deathbed, with the caption, "The days of our years are threescore and ten, and if by rea-son of strength ... ," probably because the man didn't properly learn of the benevolent social services of the German Reich when he was

---

* Plötzensee is one of the largest prisons in Berlin.

a child. Childlike old men and senile children—the artist scarcely raises his voice: he tells stories.

In the gloomiest gloom, a spark of true humor begins to glow, and oh, how Berlinish it is! "Mother," a child asks, as they're taking Father his lunch in a pail, "does that kind of sausage always grow back?" (That's how the department of natural history appears to a child.) Mudicke says, "I survived my b'loved, I survived Kaiser Wilhelm, and I'm gonna survive the Republic, too!" Amen to that. And when the landlady of furnished rooms comes in and sees her daughter lying buck naked in the flea trap and her tenant taking pictures, pedagogy, maternal dignity, and the household order are expressed in the following quiet words, "Doc, what kinda monkey biznis is that Lotte up to now?" And the good doctor explains it to her, and all is well.

Amazing, how modern the old man is. The attempt to produce a satiric newspaper—Germany doesn't have one—led on the Social Democratic side to a paper that reprinted all the old wastepaper bins from the old *Simplicissimus* and completely forgot that none of that existed anymore—not the citizens, not Mr. Baluschek, not the big-city tragedy of the old naturalists, not Serenissimi ... gone, all of it.* On the Communist side, they're still trying, sometimes successfully, but mostly not. Zille is one of the new ones, because he can be merciless and has a heart, because he depicts things mercilessly out of mercy, because he's unflappable.

You once told me you look like a horse-cab driver, Heinrich Zille. So be it. When you get ta heaven, our dear Lord'll stick some wings on yer back, put a trumpet in yer hand an' a wreath in yer hair. And then it ain't gonna be nothing but hallelujah over an' over agin. And when the people ask, "Who's that singing up there, so out of key?" I'll answer, "Pssst. He's flying around up there. Berlin's Best."

---

* Hans Baluschek, painter and caricaturist of the Weimar Republic. *Simplicissimus* was a satirical paper published in Munich from 1896 to 1944; Jewish editor Th. Th. Heine fled the Nazis in 1933.

The Lamplighters

Peter Panter, Die Weltbühne, *April 21, 1925*

Many people have probably wondered how the lamps that light the city at night are activated. Well comma the answer to this question is not difficult. Surely those posing the question have seen men moving through the streets of our city in groups of two or three—they're the lamplighters, performing the duties of their difficult job. Who are these people, and what are they doing in the dark streets at such a late hour? What requirements are there for their profession, and how are they educated? The purpose of the following lines is to enlighten the reader in this regard.

A troop of lamplighters usually comprises three men: the chief lamplighter, his deputy, and an assistant lamplighter.

The chief lamplighter leads the detachment. He shoulders the responsibility, as well as a long pole, and determines which lamps to light. After using a light meter to "shed light on" the light in the street in question, to use a technical term, he puts his team to work, as follows: When the chief thinks the time is right, the troop approaches a lamp; the chief gives the so-called "preliminary command," "Attention!" The deputy picks up the long pole and waits. The chief commands, "Light it!" and the deputy swings the lamp lever around with an expert grip. The assistant lamplighter waits with his equipment ready, for the assistant lamplighter is in charge of the technical aspects; he's the one who oversees the equipment: hammer, pliers, drill, cable, spare coal—he's responsible for all of it.

It might be difficult for a layman to fully understand the lamplighters' technical terms. When a street is thoroughly illuminated, they call it "full light." A lamplighter certainly does not "light" any lamps, but "gives light" instead. Toward morning, it's "lights out," for which the corresponding command is "lights off!" When the light levers are oiled, usually at the end of the month, the oil comes from a pot. This pot is also part of the assistant lamplighter's responsibility.

The lamplighter's education, with the exception of the assistants' mere technical school training, is purely scientific. The demands of the job are high: any man aspiring to the job must have immaculate papers, come from a family with the right political views, have participated in a voluntary maneuver with a Reichswehr brigade, and have earned top-notch grades from an upper secondary school. Training is conducted at colleges of technology, where the future administrative officials' participation in physical education is absolutely essential (forward bends, flexibility). Lectures cover: Foundations and Terminology in Light Science; History of Illumination, with special considerations for the relevant federal state; Theory of Light-Giving; Off-Lighting and On-Lighting; and Sociological Considerations in the Science of Illumination. The course of studies is followed by a national examination. After a waiting period of ten to twelve years, one is usually hired as a lamplighter, and another twenty or thirty years later, one is promoted to (no one is hired as) chief lamplighter.

As you can see, those carrying out their difficult duties in the wind and weather are elderly, expert officials. During their half century in office, they have succeeded in garnering general admiration and respect. They are members of the National Union of German Lamplighters (N.U.G.L. with independent chapters in Bavaria, Northern Thuringia, and Hamburg), and of local groups, the most significant of which is stationed in Brandenburg: the Lamp Union of Lighters in the Mark (L.U.L.M.)

These officials continually seek further education in their field—demographics, civil engineering, and traffic history. This year they finally succeeded in establishing a "Dr. Lux" degree at state universities. Continuing education for these officials is offered at Lamplighter Continuing Education Schools and Seminars; the instructors are united in a National Union of German Lamplighter Continuing Education School Teachers. Their service is not without danger; sometimes during practical exercises, a laboratory lamp gets too hot and explodes; all instructors are insured. (For details, see the "Report on German Lamplighter Continuing Education School Teacher Insurance Companies.")

Current lucifactors, as they like to call themselves, come almost exclusively from the better social strata: 65 percent of chief lucifactors and 45 percent of deputies are former reserve officers. That alone ensures their political reliability. In some families, the love of light seems to be passed down from one generation to the next; some lucifactors are third- or even fourth-generation holders of the office. The majority of assistant lamplighters, naturally, are also recruited from among military servicemen, because they typically have the "obstinacy," to use a technical term, necessary for the lucifactor profession.

Individual administrative branches are extremely interested in the lucifactors' work habits: so, just recently, His Excellency Lewald, from the National Commission on Physical Education, took part in the Fifth German Imperial Light-League Convention, even though his obligations to all other conferences that take place in Germany are quite demanding. The Reichswehrminister himself mentioned the lamplighters' thoroughly excellent work in a decree and encouraged them in the good old Sedan spirit.

Lucifactor representation in parliament is also secure; as you might recall from the last elections, Representative Dr. Pants (Bottom district) of the German National Party, a lucifactor who knows the trade from the ground up and will look after the interests of his colleagues in tried and true lamplighter spirit, was elected to parliament. He is also the one who, together with a man from the Reichswehr Ministry and Admiral Stenker from the Reichsmarine Administration, inaugurated the lamplighters' war memorial, as the lamplighters were significantly represented among the victims of the Great War and accordingly responsible for the recovery of the Fatherland. The men of light have also infiltrated the literary realm: we need mention here only Rudolf Herzog's novel, *More Light!*

The swanky N.U.G.L. National Union building is located on Berlin's Darkman Street. Since the last big opposition crisis, peace and order have prevailed within the union; Attorney Löwenstein—Jewish, but stupid, and therefore nationalistic—represented the union's interests then; now Dr. V. Falkenhayn, grandnephew of the famous victor of Verdun, has taken his place as corporate counsel. At this point, the author would like to thank the press office and its outstanding chief officer, Mr. Karl Rosner, who so kindly took the author under his wing and furnished such charming information.

Indeed, a true symbol of German strength and German industry, German drive and German loyalty: those little troops, moving almost invisibly through the streets, practicing their trying profession. Occasionally, especially in the workers' areas, the officials have been pestered by hateful, juvenile Communist boys, who call them "Night watchdogs! Night watchdogs!" But authorities have been quick to clamp down on them. The police and judges carry out their duties to protect the Republic: the culprits are always severely punished for breaking the law; imperially speaking, the German justice system has shown what it can do.

The inconspicuous appearance of these plain men hides the true sum of German activity that is to be found in them and their work. Let us hope that they continue to strive for the welfare of our nation and the benefit of the German nation, until better times come to pass, when German light will shine in Strasbourg, Gdańsk, Vienna, Budapest, and New York.

In this light, "Good light!"

Lamps can also be lit by the Central Office.

The Central Office

Peter Panter, Die Weltbühne, March 31, 1925

The Central Office knows it all. The Central Office understands the big picture, believes in the big picture, and has a map room. At the Central Office, men work together in a constant funk, but they pat you on the shoulder, saying, "My dear friend, you're in no position to judge from your individual post, but here at the Central Office ..."

The Central Office's first and foremost concern is to remain the Central Office. God have mercy on the subordinant branch that dares to do something independently! Whether it's rational or not, necessary or not, or on fire or not—the Central Office must be consulted first. Otherwise, why would it be the Central Office? Because it's the Central Office! Remember that. Let the outsiders fend for themselves!

The Central Office does not contain the intelligent ones, but it does have the clever ones. Those who do their own jobs might be intelligent, but they're not clever. If they were, they'd find ways to avoid their work, and there's only one way to do that: proposing reform. Reform proposals lead to the establishment of new departments, which—naturally—are affiliated with, assigned, and subordinant to the Central Office. One man chops wood, and thirty-three stand around—constituting the Central Office.

The Central Office is an institution designed to bewilder its subordinants' attempts at energy and activity. The Central Office thinks up nothing, and others must carry it out. The Central Office is a little less fallible than the Pope but doesn't look nearly as good.

Thus a man of action doesn't have it easy. He curses an awful lot about the Central Office, rips all of their memos into little pieces, and wipes his eyes with them. Then he marries a supervisor's daughter and gets promoted to the Central Office, for landing in the map room is *avancement*. Once there, he clears his throat, straightens his tie, unrolls his sleeves, and begins to reign: an utterly, divinely appointed Central Officer, full of deep-seated contempt for the simple men of action, in a profound, constant funk with his Central colleagues; just sitting there, like a spider in a web built by others, impeding sensible work, authorizing irrationality, and knowing it all.

(This diagnosis applies to early-childhood development facilities, ministries of the exterior, newspapers, health insurance companies, forestry commissions, and banking administrations, and is a playful exaggeration, of course, which does not apply to one company: yours.)

T. in his early twenties in Berlin, already a well-known writer then.

Berliner on Vacation

Peter Panter, Die Weltbühne, *January 19, 1926*

That thing about the hunter's cap doesn't hold true anymore, and the glasses aren't a dead giveaway either. Yet beneath the thick ulster coat, stylish jacket, and custom-tailored shirt, the old heart is still beating. But which?

There are two kinds of Berliners: the "Don't you have anything bigger?" Berliner and the "Wow, faaan-taaastic" Berliner. The second group is more disagreeable.

The fault-finding Berliner is famous. He compares everything to home, is generally unenthusiastic, and, much too apprehensive to tolerate anything foreign in silence, he spews bad jokes about everything he sees. His city invented the handy word "gripe" for such activity. This Berliner gripes.

His colleague, the "outraaaageous" Berliner, does something else, something by no means less sinister.

For about eighteen months, I've had my eye on these laudatory Berliners. When they praise something, they do it like this:

The praising Berliner exalts himself first of all when he praises. His praise, which is generally uncritical and unfounded, establishes an inner connection between himself and the object of his praise, according to the motto, "Whatever I see is good—or I wouldn't bother looking at it!" Some splendor of the object of praise thus reflects back on him, and his "fantaaastic" also applies to a select audience that can also see that this sight is worth seeing, and it contains a significant degree of contempt for the poor folk who don't see it.

The monomania of this tribe is greater than that of any other. There are dog owners all over the world who are proud of their damn dogs and puff themselves up: "But mine runs faster!" The Berliner's "aura," however, his noncorporeal body, extends much farther, to toothbrushes and underwear, cars and ink pens, to everything around him and with him … Because everything he has is well done, and there is no duplicate on the planet. He even says so. "If it's real coffee you want, you gotta come to my place!" And because the others definitely don't have the only true source for baby bottles, nor the tailor, nor the dentist, the sun shines in his universe alone. And if his neighbor has something he can't have, and he can't even participate in the adulation thereof, then of course it's all over and the object be damned. To participate in everything, understand everything, and leave nothing out: these are the three colors of his city.

Once a Berliner has given praise, there's no disputing what else might be worthy of praise, especially not then and there. "If ya didn't see it, ya didn't see anything!" Dixit.

The form of a Berliner's praise makes it clear to what extent criticism reigns supreme in this city—it always sounds like a reproach that doesn't quite apply, twisted into something friendly. "How very talented!"—how much favor, how much geniality that statement contains! Praise like that is like a fat hand waving from a lordly limousine.

But before a Berliner criticizes or criti-praises, he sits up straight in the judge's seat and is never, under any circumstances, cool and impartial. He just wants to figure it out for sure—and his pursed lips and slightly retracted chin demonstrate what the object of the critique is in for. "Well, take a look there at what you've done!" So Notre-Dame, Sacha Guitry,* the Seine, and the sun in Chantilly can all get lost.

Youth is quick to judge—? Then it would seem that the Berliner is forever young, younger, and even younger still. His terrible disposition and skittish nerves never let a single note fade away—nerve-endings twitching, he waits for the first impression, and once it's made, he sticks with it. And repeats it three thousand times—and it's impossible to get him to change his mind. "The lower body is too short," he decides after ten seconds—which functions as a leitmotiv for the rest of the evening, through conversation, critique, and dialogue, and even later, in bed, as he's turning out the light, he mutters, slightly insulted, "Yeah, but the lower body was too short …"

---

* Alexandre-Pierre Georges "Sacha" Guitry (1885–1957) was a French actor who was famous in the 1920s.

The Berliner is known to be one of the worst listeners—he wants to do everything himself. (This is why women generally can't harm him.) I always wondered why well-traveled Berliners never bring anything home with them from their trips ... Now I know. They don't listen. When the sun sets over the sea, when a man sings and a woman dances, when Paris is a silvery glow, and when the ladies from Lemberg form lively groups at night: the guy just doesn't listen. He's the character for whom, until he comes on the scene, the concept of "world" has no valid meaning. Without him, the world just isn't.

Those poor people ... They're in their own way; their bellies are an optical obstacle, and when they really want to have fun, they just look in the mirror. Their criticism is a personal, frontal attack, their praise an investiture of themselves, and you can't really go wrong, if you go where a Berliner refuses to go. Berlin is so big: four million inhabitants. Berlin is so small: a traveling Berliner won't look past the Spittelmarkt. I'll never forget what a compatriot said after four weeks' stay, the word of all words on Paris: "What kinda city is this Paris? They ain't got no chocolate cookies here!"

And the one who said that wasn't even from Berlin, so you can see how careful you have to be.

Kurfürstendamm, the main boulevard in western Berlin, in the 1920s, famous in the 1920s for its artist hangouts like the Romanisches Café, *its nightlife, and its department stores.* **Below**: *Kurfürstendamm at night.*

Berlin Traffic

Ignaz Wrobel, Die Weltbühne, November 9, 1926

The Berlin press is beating the Berliner over the head with a new obsession: traffic. The police are supporting the endeavor most effectively. It's downright ridiculous, what's being done in this city these days, to organize, statistically record, describe, regulate, divert, and attract traffic. Is there really that much? No.

When you come to Berlin, many will ask you, with practically imploring expressions, "Isn't Berlin traffic just colossal?" Now I have found the busiest times to be more like an average Parisian street at 6 o'clock in the evening, which is mediocre and nothing more. And regarding this childish bragging, I must add that I cannot comprehend the attitude of someone who can be so impressed by the quantity of traffic. At certain times of the day, there are six rows of cars side by side at the Place de l'Opéra. So? Does that make Paris any better? Does Paris gain in value because of it? It only goes to show that they didn't consider traffic like that when they were building downtown Paris, that the concentration of office districts and residences piled on top of each other is unhealthy, probably a problem without a solution, which can lead to decentralization in large cities. Those six rows of cars might prove just about anything, but nothing pleasant. You should hear old Parisians talk about the boulevards, how they used to take a short detour along the boulevards every time they went out, because it was so nice to stroll there—and today it's utter chaos, a crazy commotion, and the Parisian is happy as soon as he can get away from them. Impressive? Not in the least.

Berlin doesn't have traffic like that but imagines it does, and the police control this imaginary traffic in a way no one in Paris ever has or will. There isn't a single sensible Berlin car driver who won't admit that those gesticulating, gymnastic policemen are just a nuisance and that everything would go much more smoothly if they weren't there—and I must agree. Breaks in the traffic on Kurfürstendamm, designed to corral the wagons and send them through, are as long as those along the Champs-Elysées—except they make sense in Paris, where such breaks in the traffic are necessary, while in Berlin the breaks only serve to create concentrations of traffic that otherwise wouldn't exist.

What's so typical about this alarmingly idiotic over-organization and the fuss in the press over absolutely nothing is that this bureaucratic mumbo-jumbo is conducted purely for its own sake. The manner in which public employees, who are paid for their oh-so-important work, toot their own horns in the press these days, those prima-donna-esque performances of "the top brass"—quite a must-see!—these ridiculous overestimations of entirely simple functions appear all the more grotesque because the reality doesn't live up to all this hullabaloo in the slightest. I've often wondered what would happen in Paris if such a big to-do were made there over such trivial matters—which there might well have been cause to do. But no Parisian cares about those infinitely important questions, like whether or not the streetcar tracks will be removed from Rue Réaumur. That's rarely in the papers. Everything flows smoothly on its own, more or less; the police make mistakes or issue reasonable orders, and people have other things to worry about anyway.

This inflation of German officials, generously underwritten by the press, is taking forms that could lead one to consider whether these harmless officials aren't acting in some Metternich-era play: distracting us from what's truly essential—the state displays a colorful doll to its childish subjects, like a policeman with white signal sleeves, so everyone will sit still while someone picks their pockets.

"The green wave along Friedrichstrasse" is front-page news. The red wave coursing through the prisons, unprecedented scandals in East Prussian jails, the disgraceful treatment of illegally incarcerated Communists—of those matters there's little mention.[*]

It's not just the overcrowding, it's the urge to justify one's existence, for God's sake, by means of superfluous acknowledgment, that serves to inflate the completely unnecessary occupation of traffic cop. So nice and harmless ...

---

[*] A "green wave" is a series of green lights at crossings to make traffic flow, whereas the "red wave" T. refers to the many Communists in prison.

This whole business also accommodates the New German's intense desire to feel like he imagines the Americans to be. He can easily abstain from being a real character—but living in a town that's a "City" with a "Broadway," that really makes 'im somethin'!

You think our traffic isn't really a "problem"? Oh, but we're so problematic! Someone recently announced he'd be visiting a friend in Paris. "I'm addressing the Romance language speakers' solution to big-city problems ..." You can't get less pompous than that, and he probably won't even notice that there are no problems there and no solutions, just Paris.

What seems even more important than this artificially inflated bureaucratic stuff is keeping the administration in check. It's rather charming when the "president of corrections" gives a speech at the opening of the Hedwig Wangel Foundation—it would be even more significant if the man were to concern himself with what's happening in his department for once, with whether the most basic human rights aren't being violated there.[*]

And when those bootlicking metro editors and bureaucrats and chroniclers get confirmation of their big-city status from another thirty American women, though they're too naive to understand the meaning of such certification—one thing proves how unlike city-dwellers they really are: the fact that they strive so hard to be that way. Has anyone ever seen a Berliner make a big deal of the fact that his skin is white? You don't shout about what's obvious.

The traffic epidemic, however, is spreading across the country, and what's good for Berlin is good for Bückeburg. No cars for miles around, just two traffic cops; a car appears on the horizon, and a wild waving, tooting, and whistling ensues. The German drivers are worse than the Parisians; clumsy pedestrians and reckless drivers simply cannot coexist; it just doesn't turn out well.

Because it's not the organization that matters, but rather something entirely different, and because real life begins beyond the German's imagination.

---

[*] The Helene Wangel Foundation was a welfare organization founded in 1925 to help formerly incarcerated women. In 1926, when the article was written, there were 426,000 cars in all of Germany, according to official statistics.

Mr. Wendriner Goes to the Theater

Kaspar Hauser, Die Weltbühne, December 14, 1926

For Paul Graetz[*]

"Look, it already started!"

Treason is not inherited, my lord;
Or, if we did derive it from our friends,
What's that to me? my father was no traitor![**]

"Where's. . . where are we? Where's our row? Here? No, there! Ex-cuse me. Pardong! Sorry, thank you. Now where? Oh, there's our seat. I told you right away we should've taken the car!"

Thou art a fool: she robs thee of thy name.

"Got a program? Show me. . . I can't see anything. Who is that? No way this is Bergner. I know her; we were at a party together. . . Shush! Shush! Terrible, that people can't arrive on time! What a bum, coming in now! Just look at those legs! Why does she need to be an actress! Shush! I can't hear a thing, they're speaking so low. Very nice stage set. Yes, Reinhardt., indeed."

O my poor Rosalind, whither wilt thou go?
Wilt thou change fathers? I will give thee mine.

"Pretty dress she has on. Very pretty. . . I can't quite tell, but I think the Korders are sitting up there. Yeah, it's them; I know that numskull. Who did the music? I'll look later. Bergner hasn't been on yet, right? No, not yet. What? Intermission already? Oh, scene change.

"Just look at that—more people still coming! Nice crowd. The re-

---

[*] Paul Graetz was an actor with Max Reinhardt's cabaret *Schall und Rauch* and a good friend of Tucholsky and his girlfriend Lisa Matthias, aka Lottchen.
[**] The lines are from Shakespeare, *As You Like It*.

views were good, too. I got tickets through my brother-in-law only; otherwise I wouldn't have been able to get any. No, my wife is at the Welsches' today, playing Pritsch [bridge]. You like Pritsch? I don't care for Pritsch. Damn, I think I forgot to shut off the gas in the boiler! Look at her! I don't like her nose; but the eyes are sort of okay. Oh, it's starting again. Remind me later to tell you the joke about the ruptured appendix.

"Look—it's Bergner! I recognize her—that's her. So terrible, when the people in front of you keep jerking their heads all the time. As if it's so hard to keep your head still! How inconsiderate! Charming, isn't she. Yeah, at Tisch's place, where we saw her at a party recently, she was charming then, too. A charming person. Hey, do you remember if I mailed the letter I was carrying? I think so, right? Yeah, I think I mailed it."

Yet fortune cannot recompense me better
Than to die well and not my master's debtor

"Intermission. Very nice. Bergner is fabulous. I don't like the others much. Just listen to them clapping up there. Well? Should we go out for a while? I'm going out; are you coming? Ex-cuse me, just passing through. Shhhht! Of course it was the Korders, what did I tell you—I can tell by the butthead. Come on, let's get a beer! Hello! No idea, who that was—I know so many people. Who was that? That was him? I thought he'd look totally different. Wasn't he involved with that story about Kestenberg's affair? I don't know; she got an abortion, but he didn't want to, and then he did. . . Pretty full here! We've got pretty good seats, right! I don't like sitting in the boxes, no need to! Look, in front of us: charming person! Swell clothes, swell figure! Come on, let's go over there—goddamn fabulous! Did you see that look she gave me? My dear friend, she wasn't so bad at all. Wait a minute, my tie is crooked; there's a mirror—there. Look, she's looking again. Now that's a classy lady! Pretty good audience in general. I'm glad we got such good seats—without my brother-in-law, I wouldn't have got 'em. Look at him—gotta be an attaché, right? How scandalous, bringing such little kids to the theater! Little kids belong in bed! A classic play. . . I don't usually go to classic plays—but this one's different. Hey, look at her, that jewelry! Evening, Regierer.

So, you're here too? Yeah, so are we. What are you doing at such a good performance? I mean. . . you don't really like theater, right? Well, yes, the reviews were really good. Bergner is fabulous. I was just saying to Epstein, I don't usually like classic performances, but this one's different. Yeah, of course. Definitely. No, we went to the movies yesterday—Schepplien [Chaplin]. Quite nice. Tomorrow we're going to the Philharmonic. Left, I think, in the back aisle. Enjoy! Evening!

"You know, I don't like Regierer. Since that thing with his associate. . . what? You dunno? His associate was speculating on the side, and he didn't figure it out until he showed up at work with a new fur every day, and then there was that fuss with his son. . . yeah, the one who went to Italy with that girly—what was her name? Shht! There he is. Well, did you find it? Evening, Regierer! Evening! Have fun! Getting old, that Regierer. Oh well, the stress. . . There's a lot of illness going around these days, the flu, my wife's cousin has an enlarged spleen, the doctor still doesn't know. . . Come on, let's get a glass of beer! Don't push! You know, if you don't push here, you don't get nuthin done. How much? That's outrageous! Eighty pennies for a glass of beer! I'd like to get a piece of that action! Oh, yeah, right, I was going to tell you the joke about the rupture. So. . . and then they yell, 'Treason! Treason!' we're in the—hahahaha! Good one, isn't it? Heard it at work today. No, I haven't seen the play. Hey, you know, partisan plays—when I want that, I'll read the newspaper. Art isn't politics, you know what I mean?

"C'mon, let's check our coats. Hey, Missy, can I pick up my coat later? Here—take thirty cents. . . keep the change. Hey, do you think the gas is still on at home? That would be unpleasant—my wife gotta be home before me. There's some fluff on your suit. There's the bell. Let's go back in. Do you trade in Swiss francs? I don't know. . . by the way, Divan & Wronker just celebrated their anniversary—I had dinner there. Did you congratulate them? You shoulda—you never know. Yeah, it was a big to-do; the food was good, that dude spoke, the one from the Chamber of Commerce; Kirsch sat next to me. . . I'd love to have in the bank what he's already lost in his lifetime—come on, we should hurry.

"So, there are our seats. You know, I like to take in a play now and then. . . it takes my mind off things."

The Admiralspalast on Friedrichstrasse, along Berlin's theater mile in the 1920s. The musical and Vaudeville house is still operating today.

Confessio

Theobald Tiger, Die Weltbühne, *July 22, 1927*

We, the men from Berlin and Neukölln,
what we want, sadly, we'll never know.
For once …
For once we'll focus on just one,
and play with her alone—or none,
settle down without second thought,
even have a son, perhaps we ought,
shift our souls to function as spouse,
above the tabletop.
Generally very monogamous.
And so it was …

The others were tempting, so many dames,
they tempted us with childish indoor games.
—Ridiculous moves, significant price—
Always heeding just one bell?
Always tied to just one gal?
So shall life's hours pass, one by one?
Without any naughty fun?
Isn't the best to be found outside?

Girls? Freedom? From duty untied?
No sooner said than done.
For once …
For once we'll dance through night's wee hours,
Seem happier with this choice of ours;
sometimes barely able to grasp,
what fine ladies work with us.
And every soul who was able
lies underneath the dinner table.
Generally very polygamous.

And so it was …
Fooling around, our whole lives long?
Suddenly it seems so wrong.
Almost feverish, now we strive
for solitude and family lives.
And begin again, real men at heart,
the whole thing over, right from the start.
We, the men from Berlin and Neukölln,
what we want, sadly, we'll never know.
We torment ourselves and our women too;
they should spank our bottoms till they're blue.
Bileam's ass,* you and me.
God grant us peace for eternity.
Amen.

---

* Bileam, or Baalam, was a figure in the Old Testament, who beat his donkey because it refused to move past an angel that was invisible to Baalam. God granted the donkey the gift of speech, which told Baalam about the angel, causing Baalam to repent.

"Just a Minute!"

Peter Panter, Vossische Zeitung, *January 1, 1927*

It's a wellknown fact that a Berliner, left to his own devices, will sit staring at the ground, deep in thought, and suddenly jump up, as if bitten by a tarantula, and ask, "Is there a phone around here?" If Berliners had never existed, the telephone would have invented them. It is above them, and they are its creation.

Imagine a bold young man trying to interrupt a serious businessman during some important negotiations. He won't be able to do it. Halberds will block his path. Private secretaries will hurl themselves in front of the door; the only way through will be over their dead bodies; any attempt by that still-so-bold young man will fail. If he doesn't call. If he calls, he can disturb the President's governing, the editor-in-chief's editing, and Madam's fitting. Because in Berlin, the telephone isn't a mechanical device: it's an obsession.

When people pound on their doors, Berliners simply won't open them. But if that little phone rings, they'll dismiss the most noble visitor, mumbling in that obsequious tone usually heard only among pious sectarians, "Just a minute!" and throw themselves, keenly interested, into that little black speaker-cone. Business, midwife, stock exchange, settlement negotiations—all forgotten. "Hello? Yes? I'm__.Who are you?"

It's impossible to talk to a Berliner for fifteen minutes without being interrupted by a telephone. How many punch lines fall flat! How much built-up energy flies out the window! All that negotiative cunning, coaxing, and beautifully devious planning in vain! The telephone wasn't invented by Misters Bell and Reis*—V-Visch-

---

* Alexander Graham Bell and Johann Philipp Reis both invented the telephone, the former 1875 in Boston, Massachusetts, the latter 1861 in Friedrichsdorf near Frankfurt, Germany.

er filled the box with all its treachery.* It only rings when you don't want it to. How often have I experienced the powerful speech of some visitor convincing the entire room, approaching the summit, victory within reach, hooray, one last step ... and the telephone rings, and it's all over. The fat man at the desk, already three-fourths hypnotized, his double chin sinking down over his tie, his lower lip jutting out, relaxed, an iron mask lowering over what he passes off for a face. His hand suddenly gripping the receiver, he forgets his companion, business, and himself. "Dinkelsbühler speaking; who's this?" Zealously whirling in foreign waters, he's entirely captivated by this other, unfaithful to his companion of just a minute ago, completely submitting to deceit and betrayal.

His companion is the stupid one. He sits there vacantly, empty, the pathetic, just-uttered word dribbling pointlessly from his mouth, like an old flag in an armory, the banner of some troop long gone. He sits there, ashamed, naked and disoriented, a dull, unfulfilled desire simmering inside.

What now—?

Now the fat man at the desk talks for a long, long time, the way everyone talks on the phone in Berlin, and there's only one person talking more: the person on the other end of the line, who must be gushing like a sizable waterfall. The man at the desk gazes thoughtfully at the blotter, his eyes wander to the inkwell, stare vacantly, and then stray to the bald head of the abandoned companion. He even starts doodling, stick figures and shapes, and judging by the quivering membrane of the receiver's speaker, the guy on the other end must be shouting entire dictionaries into the phone.

The guest wriggles impatiently in his chair at the first signs that the conversation might be ending. "Well, then ... ," "All right, let's plan on it ..." The guest's spirits rise, the way a concertgoer's soul rushes ahead to the coat check when the orchestra gets ominously loud and the conductor flaps his wings to draw more and more brass into the din ... but there's still a ways to go. They continue on for

---

* In a mid-eighteen-century novel, philosopher Friedrich Theodor Vischer (a.k.a. V-Vischer) described the treachery of household objects lying in wait for the right moment to cause misfortune to their unsuspecting owners.

quite a while, heading toward the end again and again, but the end doesn't come. The waiting man feels a growing urge to hit the man on the phone over the head with the *Commercial Code*. "All right, then—good bye!" He says, and finally hangs up.

And that's the worst moment of all. The light in the deskman's eyes switches off with a nearly audible snap. He turns to his abandoned companion with a wink and a feeble expression on his face. "So, where were we?"

You start over from the beginning. You gather up the broken pieces of your conversation from the floor, take a deep breath, and try to get back into the swing of it ... good night! The momentum is gone, the cleverness is gone, and the desire is gone. The discussion dwindles lamely. You've accomplished nothing. *And this by her song's sheer power Fair Lorelei has done.*

The reader puts the book down with a quiet smile and thinks for a moment. He jumps up like a deer on the run. The *Mona Lisa* smiles up from the floor. He rushes to the telephone ...

The bus stop at Tucholsky-strasse in Berlin-Mitte, in 2012. The author is not forgotten in his hometown.

Tucholskystrasse stretches from the Spree River to Torstrasse. The Tucholsky Restaurant (below) serves traditional German cuisine today.

The Tucholsky bookstore on 47 Tucholskystrasse in today's Berlin. In addition to books, the store also sells topical items such as the pillow below.

The Slogan

Ignaz Wrobel, Die Weltbühne, January 4, 1927

In Berlin, it's like this:

This city invented collective interest. Everyone is always interested in the same thing at the same time. Curiosity, gossip, and telephone conversations all quiver to the same rhythm. The machines that set type for bold newspaper headlines are all driven by the same engine. Latent suspense, ever hovering in the wings, continually builds uniformly around a single thing at a time. Berlin is constantly issuing slogans.

Every four weeks they've all got something new on their minds, something that commands their complete attention. Only that and nothing else. One of the many characteristics of the provinciality of this city, which Frank Harris so appropriately calls the "cosmopolitan village," is that everyone is always obsessed with that one thing. Something they all get worked up about and blow out of proportion, manufacturing artificial importance. "Grock? Have you seen Grock yet? Faaantastic! We've already gone three times!" Paul Whiteman, Josephine Baker, and the police exhibit have all been *it* already. Today, *it* is *The Dictator* and Mr. André Germain;* they'll drum up something new tomorrow.

There's an intense insecurity that is specific to a certain Berlin character—always huffing and puffing in the race to keep up with the latest thing, God forbid they should fall even one nose behind!—what a pathetic sight! And when they travel to Tibet, they do so mostly out of the delightful knowledge that the competition (by which they mean everyone) hasn't been there yet. Just don't fall behind! Just be part of the in crowd!

This can't be a strong position. It leaves no middle ground and

---

* *The Dictator* is a play by Jules Romains, a nineteenth-century French playwright. André Germain was a French journalist. Grock was a very famous clown.

doesn't acknowledge that the true hallmark of a cosmopolitan is cool indifference. The average Parisian, for example, though he appears on the surface to have the daily habits of a small-town hick, doesn't fall prostrate before every Chinese attaché, and when a foreigner comes to town, the latter must first justify himself and his worth. With the French, this occasionally leads to an exorbitant self-confidence and to a voluntary limitation, about which the cleverer in the country complain. But how much nicer that is than the Berlin snob's out-of-breath fear—Me too! Me too!—of arriving too late. And because this city isn't located along the main streets of the world, it creates sensations where there really aren't any. While it's true that the city's clear and imperturbable sense of reason can't be fooled for long, the great hue and cry over mediocrity by idiots who demand a hefty experience for their money is laughable, especially because it changes every four weeks. Right now, it's something foreign. They're all dressing French.

It's certainly fine and good when the French visit the German capital and every effort is made to establish a decent relationship with their neighbors, whose benevolent neutrality is just as necessary as their airplane engines. But how childishly they go about it! What gross exaggeration! What snobby breakfasts! What flatulence with more or less mangled French grammar! Those at the Berlin salons who learn of the latest French achievements from Paris, who know how the sensible French give their authors du jour precisely that position which they deserve, will not fail to appreciate that the spiritual mother of Berlin goes by the name of Breslau. This brand of utterly uninfluential political internationalism is right on a par with that patriotic bread-ration fuss during the Great War and is a stupid party game besides, and not even the slightest bit pacifistic.

When there aren't any mediocre French authors in residence at the Adlon Hotel, the feuilleton readers find other celebrities—the kind you can be with, the kind you can get to know better. You increase your own significance by merely standing next to them, so any expense and effort is worth it when the new star generously repays it. A clown or a dancer, a movie or an Indian, a minister's wife who hosts a salon, or a cunning day-jobber. Any little characteristic that stands out, moderate qualities, pleasantly puffed up—once the Jupiter limelight of Berlin fame falls on the picture,* all the newspapers turn on the spotlight, and the new man or woman stands in the center ring, blinded and blindsided, shattered by such an economic boom.

It doesn't usually end well.

Drunk on their six months of fame, they sway under the burden of popularity and start producing sloppy work. Why bother anymore? They're well paid—overpaid. Smiling, they watch old, graying people deliver swift kicks to their own generation, regardless of their merit, just to catch even the tiniest bit of the latest glimmer of fame—the way they haughtily compare this new sunlamp with the old sun, without even a shimmer of tact, just to be in on it; the way they thanklessly forget, just to be in on it. Then comes the backlash.

A new foreigner comes on the scene, a new star, some new guy on whose genius the standard-setters all suddenly agree. Now it's his turn. The old one is forgotten. Eyes still blinded by the light of his brief fame, he sits in a dark corner and cries, unable to believe it. But he was just ... They were just calling his name, writing books about him, pointing him out to each other on the street and whispering! And suddenly it's gone. His career boom is over, and no one appreciates him anymore.

There is something unspeakably sad about this ridiculous frenzy over ever new, half-baked heroes. Like a child who wants to have a doll and plays with a pretty rag wrapped around a ball, to whom nothing is more beautiful than this doll created in the imagination. As critical and negative as the Berliner often justifiably is, this is no way to cultivate tradition. This aspect of Berlin's cultural life is best described by the posters plastered on every restaurant there:

COMPLETELY NEWLY REMODELED.

The slogans change each month, and everyone follows every one. This uniformity of thought can build up among Germans to dangerous proportions, as we all experienced with horror in 1914. When someone dares to rebel, you can swear, nine times out of ten, that he's doing so out of sheer egotism or to create a counter-slogan for some sympathetic group.

---

* Jupiter was a limelight factory in Berlin.

This runs weirdly deep. In other places, a clique follows its catchword, and no one else cares. This is why you'll rarely hear anyone boldly proclaim, "All of Paris did X." A pack of lies on the part of minor journalists. But in Berlin, the entire bourgeoisie is wearing hand-me-down intellectual fashions, and everyone looks to the next tax bracket, because no one has an internal compass. This is how Aschinger-Strindbergs and Kempinski-Freuds are made, and everything printed on fancy stationery eventually ends up at the Wertheim department store. They don't like to decide anything for themselves; someone else has to tell them. Ready-to-wear dispositions. Factory-made individuality. Mass-produced goods made to look handmade. And anything but true collectivism.

Slogans are subjugating all of Berlin.

These germs of suggestion spread through the cafés and Mrs. Wendriner's morning telephone conversations, where the celebrity of the day is cooked up. No one stays at home—everyone goes along with everything. Where would stopping and thinking get you? Whenever I see those hurried, harried, pushy Berliners, busily glancing sharply around to make sure no one has more than he deserves, or rather more than they have themselves, I remember that old man at the window of his ground-floor apartment who called to people in the lane: "There's a salmon running through the New Gate!" And he smiled to himself as they all ran to see the salmon running. When the lane filled up with the chatty, pushy crowd, he grew thoughtful, he glanced at his walking stick, grabbed hold of it, and said, "Maybe a salmon really is running … ?" And then he, too, stood in the lane.

Berlin comes up with a new slogan every four weeks, derides the old one, and is ever searching for the salmon.

Part IV
Impending Doom:
Leaving Berlin

Berlin! Berlin!

Ignaz Wrobel, Die Weltbühne, March 29, 1927

Berlin doesn't get much good press throughout the empire. The city is imitated with such malice. What's going on?

In the battle of chariots and songs, Hugenberg is one of the loud-mouths.* He got himself a couple of window dressers from the foul-smelling remains of that dirty Viennese paper *Die Stunde*, which, like Bonifacio Kiesewetters, smear the walls with strange pigments and clumsily translate their Ottakringer "Come on!" into that good ol' "Get 'im good!" Like hundreds of thousands of readers who exempt themselves when Berlin is accused of being a radical den of iniquity, while the badly aired magistrate certifies his Germanness in the provinces and Berlin is denounced as a Bolshevist nest of Jews—excepting, as always, the honorable subscriber, whom we especially refer to our advertisement section. How delightful it would be if the

---

* Alfred Ernst Hugenberg was the most influential German media tycoon of his time; he owned some forty newspapers and news agencies that delivered content to 1,600 papers, about fifty percent of the German press. He also owned ad agencies, the UFA (the main German movie studio), a bank that specialized in newspaper financing, and also defense contractors. At first, his papers endorsed the Kaiser. During the Weimar Republic, the staunch conservative, militarist, and anti-Semite became the leader of the German National People's party (see page 79). He was an early supporter of the Nazis and instrumental in helping Hitler to attain power; he was rewarded with a post as minister in Hitler's cabinet. After the war, he was interned by the Allies, but was later acquitted as a fellow traveler.

paper were only printed on rolls! Only Wilhelm the Second left that paper in its uncut condition.

So much for Hugenberg, who must realize how he happens to disturb the dealings of his people with his clumsy shouts about the "red Berlin mob." While the city on one side is trying in its seemingly odd way to organize some "tourism," without acknowledging, however, that nobody on the planet wants to pay to be treated impolitely ("prior conviction" and "foreigner" are synonyms in many a police station)—while the Tradefair Division and the Lord Mayor compete with each other—Hugenberg is hard at work on the other hand, sullying his own city and his own nest of eggs.

The provinces have other motives.

There the thought is especially unbearable, that "those people in Berlin" are know-it-alls, while local conceit, an inability to think beyond the next church steeple, and official ambition are eagerly embraced as "cultural requirements in the interest of Federalism." Berlin, Berlin!

Nor has Prussia made it easy for the people in the provinces. Berlin's superior tone, which understandably annoys the others to no end, that foolish attitude that comprises a superiority complex and hunger for power and office, has finally done some harm. Prussia's supremacy must fall, even if its government seems better put together than the imperial one. Here, by the way, we see the rare occasion when a country unconditionally knuckles down under an empire, capitulates, and then doesn't move at all. Imagine the same happening in Bavaria, which in reality is only loosely affiliated with the empire. Prussia's supremacy must fall, like that of the states, ridiculous remnants of dynastic chess maneuvers, practically devoid of cultural content; for no one can honestly tell us that the borders of the truly culturally distinct realms in Germany line up with those determined by princess prostitution and real estate deals.

Munich is dear to me—like a Little Berlin that educates its people! The anti-Berliners, who'd rather crawl into bed in their regional costumes, who can't emphasize enough their particularistic particularity, considering they clean their teeth with Kaliklora toothpaste, gargle with Odol mouthwash, use the Vaseline advertised in their newspaper, and are subject to the same effect of run-of-the-mill German advertising … Because the economy can't be fooled, and local interests (pronounced: *mélange*) end there.

Incidentally, *that* attitude copies Berlin whenever it can. Not because Berlin is so great and worthy of imitation. But it must broadly accommodate the character of the German people … The café and the bar, the magazine and the traffic light, fashion and theater, slapstick and art: practically everything, commendable or stupid, gets imitated in the provinces. Which doesn't prevent those folks from furtively fearing the infamous center of the revolution and railing against Berlin in the stupidest way. Oh, if it were only that—!

"I don't understand how someone can still be so radical at his age!" Goethe once said, as he was playing Ernst Ritter von Possart once again. Something is Goethe-ing its way through the German lands. Addicted to the gills to being one step ahead of the others, for God's sake, these cultural lifeguards smile quietly and nobly down on the "Berlin radicals." I'm not even talking about the silly nationalistic newspapers, who discover some new Teutonic genius every month or two, some sculptor who sculpts in chaste blond, holy Mother's womb, and praying warriors; a painter who steals whatever he can get from old church paintings; these days, they've gotten their hands on Hans Grimm, a fake Frenssen, when Tomback was the real one … No, we won't talk about them.*

But it's their terminology again, their stupid contemptuous posture, those feeble gestures that have the same effect as when you tie an Eastern Jew's hands behind his back when he's talking, so that he can only wiggle quietly in character … All of that can be seen all over again in fake intellectual conservatives.

Too anemic to get worked up by the times, too comfortable to risk anything, they look down, nice and superior, on those dubious, old-fashioned Berlin radicals.

To say there's not enough that's irksome, monomaniacal, or to be rejected among them is to make the German mistake: calling everything sinful except one's own group. The decorative philoso-

---

* T. is referring to Hans Grimm, the author of *Volk ohne Raum* (People without Land), which later became a Nazi slogan to justify the conquest of the East. Grimm was supposedly imitating Gustav Frenssen, also a nationalistic author.

phers, who associate "Berlin" with a radicalism that embarrasses them, can't even shoot straight: Should I … ? I can tell them how often a boastful voice and spiritual posture stand in imbalance, a phenomenon that my dear friend O. C. once christened "scribe-giants"; how snobby so much is, how unhappy these uprooted citizens are, who don't feel like re-rooted proletarians; how they sway in the wind, in need of loving care … But I'll take the last windbag among these "Berlin radicals" over some merchant's bloated son-in-law who tries to trump what moves us with moderately educated historic facts, Chinese aphorisms, and a familiarity with Viennese porcelain.

Before the war, Oscar A. H. Schmitz represented this type of philosopher with bay and every comfort—today there are many more. They're especially prevalent among adjunct professors. But when you take a closer look at what enables them to achieve such noble peace, how they come by the ability to analyze others' consciences so well, to quietly wave away shootings or even mere beatings out on the streets—it's always, always the same. They are noble, calm, and quiet because Papa's paper business is doing well; because the newspaper that employs them is selling lots of ads; because some aunty has an annuity; because they're clean, eat well, and aren't freezing—safe in the port, 'tis easy to advise. I'd rather have the uprooted middle-class son who opens his mouth too wide, whose theories are not in direct accord with his lifestyle—at least he feels what ails the world; his ear hears, his heart beats … "Protest is necessary."

I do not love Berlin. God took Berlin's Wendriners into His mouth and spit them right back out again. Its festivals are neat and tidy. Its roofs don't say to me, "Hey! You're here!" I do not love this city, to which I owe my best; we barely say hello. But when you see that cultural rubbish in every town in the empire, you have to say:

It's a childish game, this fear of dividing up bank accounts, fear of being uncomfortable, class vanity and horrible education, which sees Lao tsu* and doesn't even trip over the ill-treated prisoners, making "Berlin" a laughingstock and using it for target practice. Shit! Rot in your rotten education, oh Educated One! Drown yourself in

---

*   Lao tsu, the founder of Taoism, a philisopher in ancient China

fine formulations, Four-Eyes! Smile your superior smile—oh, how cultivated you are!

If *that's* Berlin: radicalism on military issues, absolute opposition to steel- and coal-patriotism; hating stupefaction through Reverends Mumm and Heuss;* sabotaging preparations for the next battle by War Minister Gessler, judicature, and in every school ... if all that is "Berlin," then all of us and our friends throughout the entire empire, in Hagen and on the coast, in the Mark and Saxony's industrial region, then all of us are for this city, in which there is at least movement and strength and pulsing red blood. For Berlin.

---

* Friedrich Mumm and Theodor Heuss were parliamentarians in the Reichstag, one conservative and the other liberal. Both endorsed the so-called Schmutz- und Schundgesetz of 1926, a law against smut and pornography. This led to a fierce debate; many artists, journalists, and intellectuals protested against the law, including Bertold Brecht, Alfred Doeblin, Egon Erwin Kisch, and George Grosz.

Where Do the Holes in Cheese Come From?

Peter Panter, Vossische Zeitung, August 29, 1928

The erudition of this work, which seems overcooked, compels admiration, especially in a reader like me, whose education resembles Emmentaler cheese in that it consists mainly of gaps.

–Alfred Polgar

When there's to be company in the evening, the children dine early. The children need not hear everything the grown-ups have to say; it just isn't fitting—and it's cheaper. There are sandwiches; Mama nibbles a little; Papa isn't home yet.

"Mama, Sonya said she can smoke already—she can *not* smoke yet, can she?"

"Don't talk at the table."

"Mama, look at the holes in the cheese!"

Two children's voices, simultaneously: "Toby is dumb! Cheese always has holes!"

A whiny boy's voice: "Why, Mama? Where do the holes in cheese come from?"

"Don't talk at the table!"

"But I just wanna know where the holes in cheese come from."

Pause. Mama: "The holes ... well, the girls are right, cheese always has holes ... cheese just always has holes."

"But Mama, that cheese doesn't have holes! Why doesn't it have any holes?"

"Be quiet and eat! I've told you a hundred times, don't talk at the table! Eat!"

"Wah! But I want to know where the holes in cheese ... ow! Stop kicking me!"

Big fuss. Papa enters.

"What's going on? Evenin'!"

"Oh, that boy's being naughty again!"

"Am not naughty! I just wanna know where the holes in cheese come from. This cheese has holes, and that cheese doesn't!"

Papa: "Well, you don't have to yell about it! Mama will tell you."

Mama: "You're siding with the boy? He's supposed to eat at the table, not talk!"

Papa: "When a kid asks something, I think you should just answer him!"

Mama: "*Toujours en présence des enfants!* I'll explain it to him when I think the time is right. Now eat!"

"Papa, where do the holes in cheese come from—I just wanna know!"

Papa: "Well, the holes in cheese, that's from the manufacturing; cheese is made of butter and milk, which is fermented, and it gets moist; they make it really nice in Switzerland—when you're bigger, you can come along to Switzerland; the mountains are so tall there, they're always covered in snow—neat, huh?"

"Yeah, but Papa, where do the holes in cheese come from?"

"I just told you. They come from the manufacturing, when it's made."

"Yeah, but how do they get in there, the holes?"

"Boy, stop buttonholing me about the holes and go to bed! March! It's getting late!"

"No, Papa! Not yet! Tell me first, where the holes in cheese ..."

Boom. Smack in the head. Dreadful noise. Doorbell.

Uncle Adolf. "Good evening! Good evening, Margot. Evenin', how are you? What are the kids up to? Toby, what are you yelling about?"

"I wanna know ..."

"Be quiet!"

"He wants to know ..."

"Just put the boy to bed and stop bothering me with this nonsense! Come on, Adolf, let's go wait in the living room; dinner's underway in here!"

Uncle Adolf: "Good night! Good night, you little troublemaker! Now just stop that already! What's wrong with him?"

"Margot has had it with him. He wanted to know where the holes in cheese come from, and she wouldn't tell him."

"Did you explain it?"

"Of course I did."

"No, thanks, no cigarette for me. Say, do you know where the holes come from?"

"Well, that's a silly question! Of course I know where the holes in cheese come from! They're formed during production, because of the moisture … It's simple!"

"Oh, dear, you really told the boy a load of crap! That's no explanation at all!"

"Well, don't blame me if you're being weird. Can you tell me where the holes in cheese come from?"

"Yes, I can, thank God."

"Well, then?"

"Well then, the holes in cheese are formed by the so-called casein that's in the cheese."

"That's nonsense."

"No, it's not."

"Yes it is; it doesn't have anything to do with the casein … Evenin', Martha. Evenin', Oskar … Please, have a seat. How are you? Nothing to do with it at all!"

"What are you two fighting about?"

Papa: "Please, I'm begging you, Oskar! You went to college; you're a lawyer. Do the holes in cheese have anything to do with the casein?"

Oskar: "No. The cheese in the holes … I mean, the holes in cheese come from … Well, they come from … Because of the heat during fermentation, the cheese expands too fast!"

Mocking laughter from the suddenly allied war heroes, Papa and Uncle Adolf. "Ha ha ha! Ha ha ha! Well, that's a silly explanation! The cheese expands! Did you hear that? Ha ha!"

Uncle Siegismund, Aunt Jenny, Dr. Guggenheimer, and Director Flackeland enter. Big "Good evening! Good evening! How're you? Were just talking … really funny … holes in cheese, of all things! Just about to eat … Please, you explain it!"

Uncle Siegismund: "Well, the holes in cheese come from the cheese shrinking from the cold during fermentation!"

Mumbling, increasing to rumbling, then huge full-symphonic erup-
tion: "Ha ha! From the cold! Have you ever had cold cheese? Good
thing you don't make cheese, Mr. Apolant! From the cold! Hee hee!"
Insulted, Uncle Siegismund retreats to the corner.

Dr. Guggenheimer: "Before the question can be answered, you
must first tell us what kind of cheese you're talking about. It depends
on the cheese!"

Mama: "Emmental! We bought it yesterday ... Martha, I always
shop at Danzel's now; I haven't been very happy with Mischewski
lately; he recently sent up some raisins that were ... ."

Dr. Guggenheimer: "So, if it's Emmental cheese, then it's really
quite simple. Emmental has holes because it's a hard cheese. All hard
cheeses have holes."

Director Flackeland: "Guys, you really need someone with practical
experience. You guys are all mostly academics ..." (No one argues.)
"So, the holes in cheese are a by-product of the fermentation process.
Yeah. The ... the cheese decays, because ... because the cheese ..."

Every thumb is pointing down; everyone gets up, and the storm
begins.

"Bah! I know that too! It has nothing to do with chemical formulas!"
A high voice: "Don't you have an encyclopedia?"
Stampede to the study. Heyse, Schiller, Goethe, Bölsche, Thomas
Mann, an old autograph book ... where is ... Here it is!

CALCIUM to HONEYBEE

Capital, capital gains tax, carbon, cartouche, chancellery, chap-
lain, cheese! "Let me do it! Go away! Pardon me! So:
" 'The bubbly character of some kinds of cheese stems from the development of carbonic acid from the sugar in the enclosed whey ...' "
Everyone, in unison: "There you have it. What did I tell you?"
" ... 'enclosed whey and is ... ' what does it say after that? Margot, did you rip a page out of the encyclopedia? Unbelievable.
Who's been messing around in the bookcase? The kids? Why don't
you ever lock the bookcase?"

"Why don't you ever lock the bookcase—great! I've told you a
thousand times to look ..."

"Stop it already. How did that go again? Your explanation was wrong. Mine was right."

"You said the cheese gets cold!"

"*You* said the cheese gets cold. I said the cheese gets warm!"

"But you didn't say anything about the carbonic sugar-whey, like it says there!"

"What you said was plain nonsense!"

"What do you know about cheese? You can't even tell Bolle's goat cheese from an old Dutchman!"

"I've eaten more old Dutchman in my life than you!"

"Don't spit at me when you talk!"

Now everyone's talking at once.

We hear:

"Behave yourself when you're a guest in my house!"

" ... acidic nature of the wugar-shey ..."

" ... I don't take orders from you!"

"With Swiss cheese, yes! With Emmental cheese, no!"

"This is not your house! We're decent people here ..."

"Oh, where?"

"You take that back! You take that back right now! I won't allow my guests to be insulted in my own home! You get out of my house, right now!"

"I'm happy to leave—I don't need *that* muck you call food!"

"Don't ever come back!"

"Guys, that's just ... !"

"Shut up! You're not a member of this family!"

"Well, I've never had that for breakfast!"

"And me, a businessman ... !"

"Now you listen to me: We had this cheese during the war ..."

"That's no excuse! I don't care, even if you do explode. You betrayed us, and even after I die, you'll never enter my house again!"

"Gold-digger!"

"Did you—!"

"And I'll say it again for all to hear: Gold-digger! There! So sue me!"

"You oaf! You big lazy oaf, no wonder, with your father!"

"And yours? Who's yours? And where'd you get your wife?"

"Out! You oaf!"

"Where's my hat? Gotta watch your stuff, in a house like this!"
"There will be legal consequences, you oaf!"
"Right back at you!"
Emma, who is from Gumbinnen, appears in the open door and says, "M'lady, dinner is served …"

4 civil libel suits. 2 rewritten wills. 1 dissolved partnership. 3 canceled mortgages. 3 movable asset suits: a joint theater subscription, a rocking chair, an electrically heated bidet. 1 eviction notice from the landlord.

Remaining onstage: one sad Emmental cheese and one young boy, who lifts his chubby arms toward heaven and, crying out to the cosmos, hollers: "Mama! Where do the holes in cheese come from?"*

---

* T. uses names of friends and relatives in this piece, among them Eva Sophie Sternberg, the daughter of his girlfriend Lisa Matthias on whom the character Lottchen is based, his uncle Sigmund Tucholsky; and his aunt Jenny Wiener. Gumbinnen was a town in East Prussia famous for its cheese production.

Kurt Tucholsky

Weisse with a Shot

Peter Panter, Vossische Zeitung, May 19, 1929

It was during my first two weeks in Paris—I ordered a *clacquesin* in a tavern that was way too fine for me. I shouldn't have done that. A *claquesin* is an aperitif that tastes kind of like liquid tar, but a dash more piquant. The waiter gave me a fatherly, reproachful look, not an everyday occurance with French waiters. "*Pas de goudron*," he said. We don't have any tar-drinks. I drank something lemony, like a good boy, and everything was fine.

Now, the *claquesin* is not exactly the Parisians' all-purpose elixir. But have you ever ordered a Weisse with a shot at a fine tavern in Berlin? That would be about as daring as trying to get the barber to cut your hair the way you want it ... it just doesn't happen. Fine Berlin taverns don't serve the Weisse. But why not?

The Berliner Weisse is by rights the drink of this city, and in the best of senses: pleasantly acidic, refreshing; the added sweetness of the raspberry juice doesn't really go with it but gives the thing its nice red color. Why in the world would Berlin deny itself?

Out of loathing for alcohol? That's just talk; as sensible as it is not to drink alcohol in the summer, that isn't the real reason. The real reason is: the Weisse isn't considered refined enough, and maybe it really isn't; you can't drink it out of silver mugs, and for sensitive stomachs, there are loud results ... uh, par-doan.

So we should have American drinking parlors and Hungarian wine rooms—but Berlin denies itself *itself*. It's not fancy enough for itself.

Just once—around February—the junior state court lawyer puts on a red tie and his old traveling cap and goes to the Zille-Ball.* Berlin is never less berlinerish than when it tries to be berlinish. It's really a shame.

---

* In the 1920s, "Zille Balls" were trendy parties, where Berliners would dress up as characters drawn by Berlin cartoonist Heinrich Zille.

This colonial city soaked up a little too much Austria and Prague, all kinds of compatriots from the empire, who tell it how to behave. And so the air is slightly distorted. And even if the Berliner Weisse isn't exactly a cultural phenomenon, it is a nice allegory of the city, which so rarely believes in itself. For centuries, the German has always envied others and found things "fine" just because they were foreign. Well, we don't need to tell ourselves that we aren't super-patriots … but should the idea of Berlin mean "third-class" to so many people? They want to be "like" New York. And "like" Paris. And "like" whatever else—instead of just being themselves, whereby a lot stands to be gained and little to be lost. So has the good old Berlin family gone to the dogs, like so many others, because the men just didn't have the time anymore?—But every tradition takes time and leisure and patience. It's strange: this big city has less means of expressing itself than one might imagine. Its expression is being distorted.

"For the sake of the city" is a foreign concept. You should see how the city allows itself to be represented and by whom—it's embarrassing. When they throw some money around "to promote the fine arts," you always get the feeling they're being pushed to do so—as if they don't really want to. The city has little or no sense of what is really or truly berlinish. What is Berlin doing for our Father Zille? That above-mentioned junior state court lawyer honors him at those stupid balls—and I won't go begging for that great artist—but can you believe that this city doesn't do anything, not the slightest thing for this man, who embodies the purest incarnation of Berlin?

What's truly berlinish in Berlin is hardly known, and when it is known, it's dismissed with a quiet smile of superiority, because we're just back from the Riviera … How uncertain it all is, how eternally unfinished! How insipid! Berlin doesn't lie on the Spree River; it lies on a conveyor belt.

The city does not believe in itself. Whatever lies to the east of the Spittelmarkt is *terra incognita* to the West,* which gives the city its literary expression, and those who professionally represent the

---

* The Kurfürstendamm in the western part of Berlin was home to a literary and bohemian scene, while the area east of Spittelmarkt was populated by working class folks.

term Berlin are so outnumbered by non-Berliners, that no real image can be formed. The Parisian declares his allegiance to Paris, and the Londoner to London—but the Berliner shies away from his city, because it isn't fancy enough for him, and he's much, much less of a Berliner than the man from the provinces who fights against him ever realizes.

I'm tellin' ya: dey act cosmapolitan, 'at's jus' fine; it's a big city, after all, yes indeedy—but what's really Berlin, ya know, dat, where it's warm, when ya hear it, dat, we was talkin' about, like we use ta talk about home in da trenches—don't hear nothin' 'bout dat. How many times we said in da war: man, not even a real Berlin Weisse, like da ones dat stick in yer nose 'til ya really burp … Just aks Mr. Mayor Boess—I don't think 'e ever in 'is whole life drunk a real Berliner Weisse in a real glass. Bottom's up!

Tucholsky in his thirties, in Berlin of the 1920s.

The Times Are Screaming for Satire

Peter Panter, Vossische Zeitung, June 9, 1929

For Walter Hasenclever

1

By messenger.

Dear Sir!

Assuming you might be interested in the creation of a literary type revue show with satiric overtones, we are taking the liberty of offering you the opportunity for a personal consultation with our General Director Bönheim—this very day, if possible.

We await your call between 11 a.m and 11:30 a.m..

Hoping for an immediate positive response, we greet you most sincerely,

Very truly yours,

German Literature Company, Ltd.

Department: Theater

On behalf of the Executive Director,

(sig.) Dr. Milbe

2

"Hello!"

"German Literature Company."

"This is Peter Panter. You wrote to me. Your General Director Bönheim would like to speak with me; it's about a revue …"

"Just a moment … Yes?"

"You wrote me …"

"Who is this?"

"This is Peter Panter. You wrote to me. General Director Bönheim would like …"

"I'll connect you with General Director Bönheim's general secretary."

"General secretary to General Director Bönheim speaking."

"This is Peter Panter. You wrote to me. Your General Director Bönheim would like to speak with me, about a revue …"

"Just a minute … Now what's this about?"

"This is Peter Panter. You wrote to me. Your Director Bönheim would like to talk to me, about a revue …"

'You mean *General* Director Bönheim! The General Director is not available; he's out of town. If he were here, he would be in an important meeting."

"I see, but … the letter said it was urgent … it was signed by a Doctor Milbe."

"That's the Theater Department. I'll transfer you to the Theater Department."

(Apoplexy)

Followed by: appointment with Dr. Milbe.

3

"Look, here's what I was thinking … We'll put together a revue, got it? A revue, the likes of which Berlin has never seen before! Keen, got it? Funny, witty—no doubt at all: these times are screaming for satire! It will be huge! We thought of you first … Would'ya like a cigarette? No one else will do. We'll get Pallenberg, Valetti, Paul Graetz, Ilka Grüning, Otto Wallburg—Hello? 'Scuse me a sec … (fifteen-minute telephone conversation) … So, where were we? Right, we'll get Massary, Emil Jannings, Lucie Höflich … just one little hitch—deadline for the manuscript is eight days. Has ta be! Too expensive to wait—we rented a theater. We gotta pull it off. Yeah, you can do it! Director? Piscator! Natch! Already agreed to; and if he can't, then Jessner. Or Haller. Definitely 1-A. You can count on us.

"Go to it, specially with the couplets … No, wait; no couplets. Stick with songz—these days it's songz. Not too bookish, of course, right? We want to appeal to a wide audience, so make it a little generally accessible … We were thinkin' *Threepenny Opera* with a shot of Lehár. Composers? Maybe Meisel and Kollo, or Hindemith and Nelson; it'll need a little consistency. The business end? We'll talk … our exec is at court in Moabit today. As a witness. You know, I used to dabble in literature; you know how much I envy you? How I'd love to … Hello? No, don't leave! I have more to say! (forty-five minute telephone conversation) So, we'll leave it at that, right? You'll deliver on the eighteenth, and on the nineteenth we'll start rehearsals. This way out …"*

4

"Doctor Milbe wanted to see me at half past ten."

"I'm sorry, but Dr. Milbe is in an important meeting."

"I'll wait. Hey, Mehring? What are you doing here? And you— Uncle Kästner!"

"Hi, Panter. Yeah, we've got an appointment. We met downstairs. We don't really know … Mehring told me he's working on a revue here. I'm working on a revue, too."

"Me too. That's funny—he didn't tell me anyone else would be working on this … we could have worked pretty well together … such a—"

"Dr. Milbe will see you gentlemen now."

(Hissed)—"I told you, not all three at once!"

"So, nice of you to come. I invited you all here at once—makes it simple, right? Just like we discussed. Please, have a seat. Well, we looked through your scripts, looked them over … yeah, I'm sorry to say it just won't work. Look … Hello? 'Scuse me a sec … (half-hour telephone conversation) … Where were we? Right, I was just explaining why it won't work. Mr. Kästner, yours is much too subtle—the

---

* The fictional Dr Milbe is flaunting names of show business people and artists he is pretending to hire (or have spoken to), most of them well-known in Berlin's Roaring Twenties: Actors Max Pallenberg, Rosa Valetti, Paul Graetz, Ilka Grüning, Otto Wallburg, Fritzy Massary, Emil Jannings, Lucie Höflich, and Eugen Kloepfer; musicians and composers Edmund Meisel, Walter Kollo, Paul Hindemith, Franz Lehar, and Rudolf Nelson; authors Alfred Polgar, Herman Haller, Marcellus Schiffer, Charlie Roellinhoff, and K. L. Ammer; and playwrights and directors Fritz Jessner, Erwin Piscator, and Bertolt Brecht. Quite a few of them were friends of T.. Many were later driven out or killed by the Nazis. The three not-so-fictional writers of this fictional "Revue" are Peter Panter, one of T. pseudonyms; Walter Mehring, who wrote for Max Reinhardt's cabaret *Schall und Rauch* (Sound and Smoke), a reference to Goethe's *Faust*; and Erich Kästner, a satirist and author of children's books, best known for *Emil and the Detectives*. Not surprisingly, Tucholsky did not like to write for the theater. He found it to be not only monetarily unreliable, but also fraught with an atmosphere of "fraud, hysteria, insanity, and girly talk."

people won't understand it at all ... nah, the revue should be good, but it shouldn't be too good! Mr. Panter, it's impossible, get it? Impossible—look, there, that's good, the scene with the Spreewald boat ..."

"I meant that to be a parody; that scene isn't serious ..."

"It doesn't matter—we'll make that one serious. That's the way the whole revue should be ... and here, that there—

'Get over here—Get over here with the moolah!'

"You're wrong, if you think our audience calls money 'moolah.' Sure, I get it, but this crowd'll be in tails ... and here, with the Reichswehr, that won't work at all, and that part about Zörgiebel* has gotta go ... but the rest is really ... Hello? Scuse me a sec ... Dammit! I'm in an important meeting! Don't bother me now! No! Yes! I don't know! Listen!" (half-hour telephone conversation) Now where ...? Right, Mr. Mehring, don't take this the wrong way—I didn't get it! I just don't get it! Well, I don't have the literary education you do ... at least I earned my journalistic stripes; I wouldn't dare give that to General Director Bönheim—he'd laugh his head off! Look—

And because the Eskimo doesn't talk like the broker:
That's why no one, none of us, understands each other!'

"Get it? Of course he talks different. And that part, there—

There's a corpse in the Landwehr Canal.
Fisherwoman, you little ...'

"First off, that's old—and besides, it's unappetizing; the audience will want to eat after the show. No, guys, that just won't work. So, just rework it for me ... you know? Nutty, funny, witty; I'm meeting with Mr. Polgar and Mr. Marcellus Schiffer and Roellinhoff this afternoon. We've gotta get this done! Or else I'll go to Mr. Ammer or Villon, or, worst-case, Mr. Brecht ... So, meet me at four, gentlemen, at the director's ... Bye bye!"

---

* Karl Zörgiebel was an infamous Berlin police commissioner of the 1920s, under whose watch the police shot and killed rioting workers.

** A reference to the poem "Wiegenlied" by Walter Mehring, which combines the traditional folk song "Little Fisherwoman" with a verse about the killing of Rosa Luxemburg, a famous Jewish Communist leader who was killed by right-wing militias; her corpse was thrown into the Landwehr Canal.

5

"I told him, I won't do the production at all. I don't know why he told you all to meet me here! *If* I do it, it will be under the following conditions: Convictions! Convictions! Convictions! There has to be something in it about the housing shortage. There has to be something in it about the repeal of Paragraph 194 of the Code of Criminal Procedure—those are problems! And then there's the film."

"What film?"

"The film version of Bronnen's play."

"What Bronnen play?"

"That play about the novel by Remarque.˙ The film about the play about the novel—we're making a talkie out of it—not really a talkie, but it'll have an escalator. Jessner has ... Good afternoon, Doctor! Good afternoon, Director Bönheim—so nice of you to come ..."

"Where can I make a call?"

"Here you go ..."

"Right. Let's begin. OK, so, gentlemen, we'll start rehearsals tomorrow, but we'll need to make a few little changes first. This part—hand me that—this won't work. We can't make so much fun of the justice department. That's gotta—hand me the red pen, thanks!—that's gotta go. Gentlemen, in case you didn't know, we're affiliated with Bosenstein & Klappholz, and IG Farben backs them, so jokes like that about the stock market ... no, tasteless, I'm sorry, but we don't want to do that. Just stick to being nice. And here, that part about the 'Internationale,' they can sing that, if you want; people like to hear that before dinner these days. So rework that for me—"

"Phone call for General Director Bönheim!"

"For me? 'Scuse me a sec!"

(Unsettling pause. Whispering.)

"Doctor Milbe means ... with Fritzi Massary!"

"You go ahead and do that, Panter; you've always wanted to do couplets—no, thanks, I don't smoke anymore—for the gal ..."

---

* Erich-Maria Remarque's book *All Quiet on the Western Front* is a landmark anti-war novel. Arnolt Bronnen was an Austrian expressionist turned Nazi turned Communist whom T. regarded as a commercial hack. A Bronnen play based on the Remarque book would not be a good fit.

"So, I'm back. Right, I just found out that Emil Jannings said no, by telegraph, and Otto Wallburg, too. No harm done; we'll just reshuffle the cast; I've got a couple of very talented young people. (Milbe, I'm thinking of … pssspssspsss …) Right, so how far have you gotten? With the deletions. Yes. Mr. Mehring, what did the Reichskanzler ever do to you? Leave the poor man in peace—his life can't be all that easy. Right? No, look … Berlin traffic regulations, for example—now that's scandalous! Just now, in my car, I had to wait five whole minutes at Wittenbergplatz—you should write something about that! Right. And the title?"

"Yeah, the title … ?"

"Mr. Kästner, what did you call it?"

"Heart in the Mirror."

"And you, Mr. Panter?"

"Sweden-punch."

"And you, Mr. Mehring?"

"Night on the Brocken."

"Right, great—then the revue will be called 'Everybody should visit Berlin.' Gentlemen, Doctor Milbe will explain the rest; I've got an important meeting. Goodb—"

"Of course, General Director. Fabulous, General Director!"

"So, gentlemen, as I said: the revue will go on—just rework it!"

6

"Stop!"

"Why stop?"

"Why is there an alligator on the stage?"

"At my request—Mr. Klöpfer wants it that way …"

"But that doesn't have … . that doesn't have anything to do with the script! It's the matchmaker's song … what has that got to do with anything? …"

"I'll drop that r-r-role right on your feet, if Mr. Panter won't stop bothering me! To hell with rehearsal—I can't … There—"

"But Mr. Klöpfer … we …"

"Shut up! I'll str-r-rangle you with my bare hands! If I don't make something out of this bloody script, not a single soul will laugh—no one will even come to see it! All the nuances come from me— everything is me. Here, that bit about the tires, and during the second refrain I'll leave the wrong way and come back with a gas mask, and if I can't pick up the alligator, then you can all just ..."

"Mr. Panter, just let him have the alligator! It could be really good! (Piano:) This evening I'll give the beast some castor oil!"

7

"I won't sing that."

"Well, kids, if you don't sing what's written there—you can't just make up your own verses!"

"And why can't we? We can do it really well! You'll just have to write us a better script, Panter-Baby!"

"My dear lady, that just won't do. I don't care what usually gets sung around here, but my name is on the page ..."

"I can't do it! I can't do it! My nerves won't take it! I'll throw the whole thing out! Either I'm singing here, or I'm not! You get out of here, you old horn-dog—the whole day long, the guy has been after Kate ... no one's working here ... I'm surprised you didn't bring your beds to the theater!"

"Hey, kiddo, it's ..."

"This brothel is a theater ... I mean, this theater ... I'm leaving! Play your own rubbish!"

8

"Clear the stage! Wait, no! Don't start yet! What's wrong, Mr. Director?"

"Milbe, rework that for me! There, that bit in the fourth scene. Impossible! How could you leave it like that! Foreign Minister Stresemann is a frequent visitor at the theater club; you can't mess around with our diplomacy like that! Commerce Minister Moosheimer has already got on my back for getting involved at all—I already dread this whole revue ... and, uh ... and then the cops can't be putting their uniforms on again in scene eight; they'll have to put on French uniforms; we've got some left over from the last revue ... have Pichorek check on that immediately—and the song against the Reichstag will be omitted ... that ..."

"But it worked quite nicely during the dress rehearsal, Mr. Director!"

"I don't give a shit! Who's the director here?—you, or me? Those revolutionary texts—I'm a good Weimar Republican ... the caricature of the crown prince in the court scene has also got to go; it's easy to kick a dead lion, and I don't want to lose all my business connections because of you; besides ..."

"Clear the stage! Gong—ah!"

9

(*Deutsche Tageszeitung*): "Red Rubbish"

(*Vossische Zeitung*): " ... our friend Peter Panter may well have had a bad day. It happens to everyone. But on days like that, you shouldn't write anything. After the scene at the Reichstag, which was oddly bland, the speaker departed, and we were left wondering what it was all about; then it seemed as if the actor playing the Reichstag president had something to say, but the author's creative juices had run out ... and what business French policemen have in a German assembly hall is likely to remain the author's secret ... it just wasn't his day. Throw this beast of prey a different kind of roast and it will jump through new hoops."

10

(Mrs. Wendriner on the phone, half past ten in the morning)

" ... she said she'll give you a call when she has another maid for you. You can depend on her; she always finds me teacups to match my dishes. She's totally dependable. Yesterday? At the Majolika Theater, for the new revue. Premiere. Uh-uh; so-so. Bois' acting was pretty nice, but it was all really confusing—we didn't laugh a bit. It was supposed to be this really big thing, but we wanted to leave by intermission. Oskar stayed, 'cause he wanted to talk to Paul after the show—'bout business. The only good part was Graetz and Hesterberg, but nothing else. Margot called yesterday, wondering why you never call her. She'll call me again tomorrow, and you should call Lina, too, to tell her to call Trudy about the lacquer; Katy is pretty happy ..."

*The Deutsches Theater in 2012, where this satirical revue could have tak-
en place. In the foreground: A statue of famed director Max Reinhardt.*

11

"It's your fault!"

"Me? That's just great! It's your fault!"

"Who told you so? I told you so!"

"Stop making such a big fuss in the theater office! That won't bring the money back! Instead of getting decent authors! Presber! Remarque! Ferdinand Bruckner! Noooo, you had to haul in your good friends …"

"I won't stand for it."

"It's not your place to not stand for it—this is my operation, Doctor Milbe! Why are you all just standing around? Are you waiting for money from me? You want money for that? You tell me why I paid to rent the theater … I just wanna tell you to—"

"What kinda tone is that?"

"You're fired! You, too! I'll clean this place out with an iron broom!"

"Kiss mine! This shit-hole of a theater—that's it!"

"Get outta here! He's got the character of a toilet seat …"

"Panter! Go! Get out!"

"But you …"

"I …"

"You big idiot! Who's been telling you from day one? But nobody listens to me, in my own company … from now on … I'm an old hand in the theater, and these young rogues these days … I'll just sell the company; you'll see how you'll get along without me! I'll go to the talkie syndicate, or back to apparel!"

"On your way out? I'm on my way up—to get my money."

"Don't even bother. There's no money up there. Just trouble."

"Dear God … what's going on up there? Who's hollering like all hell's breaking loose?"

"That? That's just these times—they're screaming for satire!"

In the Hotel Lobby

Peter Panter, Vossische Zeitung, August 10, 1930

One look—and the nose sits in the back

We were sitting in the lobby of a big hotel, in one of those lobbies that always look like they do in the movies—the movies won't have it any other way. It was five minutes to five thirty; my companion was a neurologist; his office hours had ended; and we were drinking weak tea. It was so expensive you could even have said we were *taking* tea.

"Look," he said. "It just takes practice. They come and go—men, women, Germans and foreigners, guests, visitors ... and nobody knows them. I know them. One look—delightful, if you've learned a thing or two about psychology. I leaf through these people like an open book."

"What are you reading now?" I asked him.

"An extremely interesting chapter." He glanced around, through squinting eyes. "No mysteries here—I know them all. Just ask me."

"All right ... Who's that man there, for example?"

"Which one?"

"The old man ... with the sideburns ... no, not him—that one over there."

"Him?" He didn't pause for a second. "That's ... that man, as you can see, bears a striking resemblance to old Emperor Franz Joseph. You might even say he's the spitting image of the emperor—he looks like ... he looks like an old mailman, someone people think is kind because he brings them their monthly pension checks. His posture—his airs ... I think he's a former court official from Vienna—a rather important one, at that. The collapse of the Habsburgs upset him, even upset him a lot. Yes. But look at the way he's talking to the waiter: that's an aristocrat. No mistaking it. An aristocrat. Just look—inside that man is the Ballhouse Square, Vienna, the entire culture of old Austria, the Spanish Riding School—*tu, Felix, Austria ...* * he's surely some 'His Excellency'—some huge big shot. That's who he is."

"Stunning. Really. Stunning. How do you know all that?"

He smiled, too flattered really to be flattered. How vain must this man be! "Like I said: practice. I picked it up during my consultations. I'm no Sherlock Holmes—certainly not. I'm a neurologist like any other—just with an eye for such things. The eye." He took a drag on his cigarette, satisfied.

"And that woman back there? The one sitting at the table, she seems to be waiting for someone—look, she keeps looking at the door ..."

"Her? Dear friend, you're wrong. That woman isn't waiting. At least she isn't waiting for someone here. She's waiting ... yes, she is waiting. She's waiting for a miracle. Wait ... just a minute ..."

He pulled a monocle out of his vest pocket and stuck it in place. It wasn't quite right, so he adjusted it.

"That's ... Yes, that's one of the few great courtesans left in this poor world. You know, don't you, that courtesans are dying out like the word due to the petty-bourgeois competition ... Yes, what I mean is a queen of lust-for-hire. Less pathetic: a great, truly great madam of the *demimonde*. Damn ... did you see that hand gesture? She devours men. She devours them. She's really ... And those eyes, look right in her eyes. . . look right inside them ... you can see a grief complex in those eyes, an entire garden filled with weeping willows. That woman is longing; after so much unfulfilling fulfillment, she's still longing. No doubt about that. I doubt she'll ever find what she's looking for. What she wants is so difficult—very difficult indeed. That woman had everything in life—everything. And now she wants more. That won't be easy. That veiled moll! Maybe some man committed suicide over her—maybe—I can't really say now for sure. I'm not omniscient. I'm just a doctor of souls ... I would like to have loved that woman.

---

* *Bella gerant alii, tu felix Austria nube!* (Others fight wars; you, happy Austria, marry!) describes the attitude of the Austrian empire. Ballplatz, or rather Ballhausplatz, is a place in Vienna where the famed opera houses are located.

Understand me—not to love! *To have loved.* Loving that woman is dangerous. Very dangerous. Yes, indeed."

"Doctor … you're a regular Cagliostro … !* Your patients should definitely take you seriously!"

"Nobody fools me," he said. "Not me. What else would you like to know? While we're at it …"

"That man there! Yes, the fat one who's just standing up—he's leaving—no, he's coming back. The man with the reddish face. What's his story?"

"Well, what do you think?"

"Hmmm … today they all look alike … maybe …"

"They all look alike? You just can't see. You just can't see. The ability to see is everything. It's really very easy."

"Well?"

"That man is a wine merchant. Either the boss himself or the buyer for a large wine company. An energetic, educated man; a strong-willed man, a man who rarely laughs and doesn't think much of humor, despite the wine. A serious man. A man of business. Relentless. Hates large gatherings. A solemn man. That's who he is."

"And that woman there? That petite, ordinary-looking lady?"

"Panter, how can you say such a thing? That's—(monocle out) that's a good, respectable housewife from the provinces … (monocle back in the barn)—a good woman, mother to at least four children, raised in the stern grip of a lower-middle-class family—goes to church every Sunday, cooks for her husband, mends her brats' dresses and pants. Everything is in order. *She is loyal and true and strays not from God's path*, or so the song goes … not her."

"And that man there, Doctor?"

"You see—now that's the typical money man of our time. There you have him. I could tell you his life story, so clear is that man's soul laid out before me. A money-grubber. A tough guy when the going gets tough. He won't let anyone get him down. Doesn't sweat the small stuff; doesn't read books; doesn't give a damn about anything but his business. There you've got an Americanized European. With

---

* Alessandro Cagliostro, whose real name was Giuseppe Balsamo, was a famed Italian alchemist, occultist, impostor, and con artist in the eighteenth century.

the women—good God! It's six … Forgive me, but I have an urgent appointment. I'll have to take a cab. Hey, gimme the bill!—uh, I mean, May I have the check please?"

The waiter came, took, and left. The doctor stood up.

"What do I owe you?" I asked in jest.

"Priceless, priceless. Take care! So … see you soon!" And he was gone.

I was overcome by curiosity, completely overcome. All of the analyzed victims were still there—every last one. I made my way over to the hotel porter, who had a good view of the lobby from his position. And I spoke with him. And I slipped something into his palm. And I asked. And he answered. And I listened:

The Austrian courtier was a sewing machine dealer from Gleiwitz. The great whore with the grief complex was Mrs. Bimstein from Chicago—and her husband had joined her at the table, unmistakably Mr. Bimstein. The buyer for the big wine company was Grock the Clown. The chubby mama was the owner of a hospitable *établissement* in Marseille. The impudent money man was a poet from the avant-garde German school—

And only the psychologist was a psychologist.

Lottie Confesses 1 Lover

Peter Panter, Vossische Zeitung, January 23, 1931

"I smell strange? What's that supposed to mean—I smell strange? I don't smell strange. Give Lottie a kiss. The whole four weeks you've been in Switzerland, nobody's given me a kiss. Nothing happened here. No—really, nothing happened here! What did you notice right away? You didn't notice anything right away ... oh, Daddy! I'm just as true to you as you are to me. No, what I mean is ... I really am true to you! You fall in love every time you hear a song with a woman's name in it ... I'm true to you ... Thank God! Nothing happened here.

" ... Just a couple times in the theater. No, cheap seats ... well, once in a box ... How do you know? What? How? Who told you that? Well, those seats were ... through connections ... Of course I was there with a man. What, I'm supposed to go to the theater with a nun? ... Dear Daddy, it was completely harmless, totally harmless, don't make it like in the Camorra or Mafia or whatever they do in Corsica. In Sicily. Whatever! Anyway, it was harmless. What did they tell you? What? Nothing happened here.

"That was ... that's ... you don't know him. No, I wouldn't do that—if I go to the theater with another man, it's not gonna be any man you know! Excuse me, but I did not compromise you. Men are so stupid; they hold it against you if you do something with a colleague from work. And if it's not a colleague from work, then right away it's 'Miss Julie!' You just can't win! So you don't know him! You don't know him. Yeah, he knows you. Hey, be happy so many people know you—you're famous. It was completely harmless. Totally. We went out to eat afterward. Nothing else.

"Nothing. Nothing happened. The guy ... the guy is just ... I took him along in my car, 'cause he looked so nice sitting next to me ... a dazzling beard—did Reventlow tell you that, too? Well, that's what I call it too. But he just was a beard. The guy was gorgeous. Really, it's true. A wonderful mouth, such a hard mouth—give Lottie a kiss. He was stupid. Nothing happened.

"He wasn't completely stupid. It's just … I did not fall in love with him at all; you know perfectly well I only fall in love when you're around—so you have your fun too! A nice guy … but I don't want those guys anymore. Not me. I don't want any of it anymore. Daddy, he wasn't really all that good-looking. But he was a good kisser. Just that—nothing else happened.

"Hey, who do you think I am? Do you think I'm like I think you are? You, I won't put up with it! I am faithful. Daddy, the guy … it was just kind of a mood. Yeah, first you leave me alone here, and then you don't really write, and you only call once—and when a gal's alone, she's more alone than her guy is. I certainly don't need a man … not me. I didn't need him, either; he shouldn't go around thinking that! I just thought … .I thought, when I saw him … I knew right from the moment I saw him—but it wasn't anything.

"After the theater. Then for two weeks. No. Yeah. Just flowers, and candy, twice, and that little soapstone lion. Nope. My house key? You're crazy … ! I did not give him my house key! I don't go around giving strange men my house key! I'd rather take him down to the door myself. Daddy, I didn't feel anything for him—and he didn't for me—you know it's true. 'Cause he had such a hard mouth, and really thin lips. 'Cause he used to be a sailor. What? On the Wannsee? The guy went to sea—on a huge ship, I can't remember the name, and he knew all the commands, and he had a hard mouth. Really thin lips. Man, he doesn't talk much. Kisses good, though. Daddy, if I hadn't been feeling so down, it wouldn't have happened … Nothing happened, really—that doesn't count. What? In town? No, not at his place; we ate together in town. He paid—hey, did you see it? Am I supposed to finance my acquaintances … really … ! It was nothing!

"Tattooed?! The guy wasn't tattooed! His skin was totally clear; he had … No details? No details! Either I'm supposed to tell you, or I'm not. I won't tell you one thing more about him. Daddy, listen—if he hadn't been a ship's mate, or whatever it's called … I will tell you this:

"First off, it was nothing, and second, you don't know the guy, and third, 'cause he was a sailor, and I did not give him anything, and besides, like Paul Graetz always says: Just when you've got it, then you're—Daddy! Daddy! Wait … what is this? What? How? What kind of picture is that? Who is that? How? What? Where did you meet her? How? In Lucerne? What? You went on outings with her? Don't tell me everyone goes on outings in Switzerland. What? Nothing happened?

"That's totally different. Yeah, I like a guy now and then. But you men? You'll throw yourself at anything in heels!"

Lisa Matthias, whom T. made famous as "Lottchen" (Lottie). He wrote a series loosely based on her.

Alexanderplatz in the late 1920s, on the brink of modernity,
when two new subway lines were built.

In Defense of Berlin

Peter Panter, Vossische Zeitung, May 4, 1929

Recently I wrote here about the people who live on the margins of prosperity.

"One might wish," a reader wrote, "that you would scrutinize not only those on the brink of prosperity, but prosperity itself, in all its vanities. Members of those social circles where it's an embarrassment to fall behind the trend in even the most trivial way ... such characters thrive exclusively in the petri dishes of Berlin. If those of us who live out in the much-chided provinces refuse to model ourselves on this society, then no Berliner should be surprised that he is and ever will be a caricature everywhere, save in his metropolis, and that not one among the ranks of civilized provincials dreads anything as much as encountering Berliners."

And there you have it.

*

First off, both sides are terribly wrong.

Berlin is wrong when it chides the provinces. The provinces aren't all as provincial as big-city dwellers like to think; Germany is in the enviable position of being a decentralized country; so while there is no Little Paris in France, we have many cultural centers out there in the provinces. The "provinces" you might find in a farce might exist, but the majority of large country towns cannot simply be tossed into the same big pot labeled quirky small-town originals. That's just plain wrong. And the provinces, with their distorted view of Berlin, are wrong too.

There are wealthy upstarts and rich snobs everywhere; the fact that there are more of them in a big city than in Magdeburg is not an argument against the big city. What exactly has the Berliner done to the provincial?

His recompense—as stated above—is the provincial's wistful

resentment at not being able to live in Berlin, and this longing—despite the whole admiration thing—is so wrong!

"The theater! Intellectual stimulation! There's so much to see!" Very nice. But these admirers are forgetting that such credits go hand in hand with considerable debits: slaving away, ten times the tension, that "amounting to nothing" for which not only the big-city dweller, but the big city itself is to blame. Berlin surely has the best theater in the Reich—but man cannot live on that alone. And no one is as hard on the provinces as the provincial himself.

Bernard Shaw once pointed out that the man who groans so heartbreakingly about his family does them an injustice—along the lines of: "Uncle Franz, who so stupidly collects stamps, is a type to be found everywhere, not just in your family; the jealous Hilda and the monotonous Frieda, and the overambitious Eugenia, and the pedantically dense Papa—the whole world is composed of people like that, and in your small world you have the big—oh, stop complaining!"

"All we have," the provincials complain, "is farmers and religious zealots and little people and racketeers and philistines …" And in Berlin? Do the provincials really fail to believe that every single circle in Berlin has those things too? They're just more evenly distributed; they have stronger opponents, and balance is more or less maintained. Berlin is not inhabited by angels.

But not by devils either. What the Hugenberg press dished out in this department, against the better judgment of the editors involved, went too far. Even country squires know pretty well that the Berliner does not just sit in a bar and drink all night and dance with the staff in heavy makeup; that preoccupies no one as intensely as the gentlemen at the *Grüne Woche*—the agricultural fair—and the propagandists against Berlin's most vital interests are loyal family men who know for a fact that people do work in Berlin and just how much they work—but they are forced to manufacture a wanton Berlin life for the quivering provincials, though they can barely picture one themselves.

Because you do have to know Berlin well to be able to scold Berlin. The funny thing about Berlin's rich, medium rich, and wannabe rich is … we know what it is. And we have never been ashamed to say it. Germany, however, is not a picture in black-and-white—the good provinces out here, and the bad Berlin over there. That doesn't work. The fact that Mt. Hugenberg screwed up more than all the tourist centers can make right again is something that those involved will have to work out among themselves—but Berlin's reputation is truly inaccurate. It has—like any circle of people—its faults; but much, much different ones from what the provincials believe them to be. Some smart Berliner should really get a handle on this propaganda against Berlin ...

The man standing in front of the Cologne Cathedral, remarking gruffly and piously, "Ain't got nothin' bigger?" may come from Berlin, but his reaction comes from a state of mind that is indigenous not only to Berlin. I think that pitting the provinces against Berlin leads us nowhere, because it arises from the false assumption that the provinces are something homogeneous, while the only thing that a Lower Bavarian county seat and a Friesian village have in common is the fact that they're not Berlin—and that's not enough to unite them.

Germany consists of associations. Is there no "National Association of German Provincials" yet? Just you wait. "Let's send them to Hagenbeck," as the Swedes say—both the Berliner—who tells foul jokes (because they're bad) about the provinces, which he knows nothing about—and the provincial. And let's try to understand each other, Berliner and provincial. As for the Berliner, if he's funny and ridiculous and a laughingstock ... I possess enough local pride that I want to make fun of him until the cows come home. Out of love, my dear reader from Bitterfeld.

Unless the Berliner is berated, he won't learn.

Brief Outline of the National Economy

Kaspar Hauser, Die Weltbühne, *September 15, 1931*

A national economy is when people wonder why they don't have any money. There are many reasons for this, the best of which are the scientific reasons, though these can be quashed by an emergency decree.

The old national economy was simply laughable, so we'll just skip over it without a word. It reigned from 715 b.c. through the year after Marx. Since then, the issue has been thoroughly resolved. Though the people still don't have any money, at least they know why.

The basis of all national economies is what is generally referred to as "money."

Money is neither a means of payment nor a means of exchange, nor is it fictitious; above all, it is not money. With money, you can buy goods because it's money, and it's money because you can buy goods with it. Meanwhile, this theory has been abandoned. Where money comes from is not known. It's just there or not there, and usually not there. Paper money in circulation is guaranteed by the state; this means that anyone possessing paper money can go to the imperial bank and demand gold in return for his paper. Yes, he can. The senior officers at the national bank are required to have gold fillings, which guarantee the paper money. This is called gold-backing.

The affluence of a country is based on its balance of trade surplus/deficit, on its domestic and foreign loans, and on the difference between the giro of the exchange premium and the interest rate of the collateral loan; when it rains, the opposite is true. Every morning, the national banks roll the dice to determine the so-called "discount." Just recently, the Germans succeeded in rolling a 20 with just three dice.

Regarding the world economy, it is interconnected.

When wares leave the businessman through a sale, they no longer have value, but are rubbish; the businessman, however, has the money, which is called added value, although it's worth less and less. When a businessman is bored, he calls some others and they form a trust, which means they commit to no longer producing any more than they are able and not to sell their wares below cost. That workers must receive wages for their work is a theory that has been generally abandoned today.

Exports play an important role in trade; an export is when others are supposed to buy what we can't buy. It is also unpatriotic to buy foreign goods; for this reason, foreigners must consume domestic (i. e. German) goods, because otherwise we will not be competitive. When an export goes the other way around, it's called an import, the plural of which is cigars. Because cheaper wheat is unhealthy and not as easily digestible as the more expensive rye, we have protective tariffs, which protect the tariff as well as the German agricultural industry. The German agricultural industry has lived for twenty-five years on the brink of disaster and feels pretty much at home there. It's in debt, because steel and coal leaves nothing to spare, and steel and coal is not on top, because the agricultural industry takes too much away from it. This is called balancing interests. Both institutions are subject to high taxes, which the consumer must also pay.

Every economy is based on the credit system, which is the erroneous assumption that others will pay back borrowed money. If they don't, the result is a so-called "rescue operation," in which everyone except the government turns a good profit. When the public is asked to have some confidence, it's known as bankruptcy. Indeed, they usually don't have anything more than that.

When business owners secure all of the money abroad, it is called a serious situation. Well-structured governments can easily deal with such a situation, unlike in the smaller pirate states, where bands of robbers suck the impoverished population dry. Corporations are also an important component of the national economy. The shareholder has two important rights: he's the one who supplies the money, and he can join the opposition at the general meeting and have something put on record that the board treats as a so-called shabbos. Corporations are essential to the economy: they create the preferred stock and seats on the supervisory boards. Every corporation has a supervisory board, which advises on matters that it should actually be supervising. The corporation holds the supervisory board responsible for the timely payment of profit percentages. The excuses a corporation has for why it can't pay any taxes are compiled in a so-called "balance sheet."

The economy would not be the economy, if we didn't have the stock market.

The stock market is where a bunch of excited men go instead of the casino and the restaurant; the pious also go to the synagogue. The stock market assesses the global situation at noon each day, in accordance with the bank directors' vision, though they can rarely see beyond their own noses, which can actually be quite a long way. If the people yell at the stock market more than usual, it's called a steady market. This is followed—the next day—by the public coming and getting involved, once the best stuff has already been extracted. If the market is weak, the public is always involved. This is called customer service. The stock market fulfills an economic function: without it, jokes would spread much more slowly.

In the economy, there are also smaller employees and workers, but these have long since been dropped from the new theories.

In summary, it can be said that the national economy is the metaphysics of the poker player.

I hope my explanation has been of use to you, and I would like to add that it is offered just as all goods, contracts, trades, promissory notes, and other business commitments are: without any guarantee whatsoever.

Mr. Wendriner Lives in a Dictatorship

Kaspar Hauser, Die Weltbühne, October 7, 1930

To be spoken in a low voice

"Shush!

"I told ya not to talk so loud. There's SA guys outside the movie theatre … see 'em? How much? It ain't gonna rain … it'll hold off. C'mon in. And shut yer mouth. 'Scuse me, please … Now hush up. What've we got? First row—swell! So, coat goes there; yours … gimme that. So.

"Commercials. That's a commercial Hey, we already saw that one—that's … Regierer! Hey, that's funny! What're you doin' here? What, in the box seats? Well, well, fancy folk … ha ha ha … So, are those tax cards? Well? Hey, Regierer's got two tickets he ain't gonna use. Welsch is comin', too. Let's go on up to the box. Wait, we'll come over to you … here, take my coat. So, at least we can talk here.

"That was just the newsreel. Parade in Mecklenburg. Pretty crowded, huh? Lotsa military here. Ya know, ya really miss something when they're not around. Yeah, you're so used to it … Ya see some really fancy appearances among 'em, by the way. God, I think it's mighty nice. Right, Hanne? Downright festive. Yeah. Hey, Regierer, whaddaya think? What? We'll just see? That's what I always say. Ya know, I don't think it's all that bad. When was the last time we talked? Two months ago … in September … Yeah, look … remember that big panic then? Such a relief since then … At least we know where and how. Yeah, that was some kinda mood then … my wife sent me to bed for four days, I was so run-down. And who coulda predicted that? You couldn't see a thing here on Kurfürstendamm before! Nope. Look, there's Gebühr, Otto Gebühr. Those French supposedly just made him some kinda proposal—he's supposed ta play Napoleon. He didn't accept. He'll just play Doctor Goebbels, he said: the right perspective. Yeah. Did Welsch really vote fer the Center Party? Meshugge. I'll ask him later. Anyway, it really ain't so bad. I heard from a business buddy from Rome, told me we're downright free compared ta them there, he did. You got a yellow permit too, right? Course we got a yellow permit. Ten years? I been livin' in Berlin for more than twenty years; I got one right away ... Intermission! Shush! Look at the black guy down there! Probably an Eastern Jew ... Ya know, anti-Semitism sure is justified against them. I think so too. Just look at that! Disgusting. Surprises me he's still here and they ain't deported Æim yet!

"Yeah, I can't complain. Strict order in effect on our street ... we got a real nice SA man on the corner, such a nice guy ... Every morning, when I go ta work, I give 'im a cigarette—he always salutes when he see me coming; salutes my wife, too. What happened ta you? What did Regierer say? They knocked his hat off? What for? Yeah, my friend, you better raise your arm! With the flag bein' our national emblem, I figure you better salute it too.

"Shush! Powder keg! Powder keg! You think I'm sure? Every mornin' my wife calls me at work ta find out if somethin's happened. Nothin' yet. That was real good, just now. Did'ja see that? The way he acted blind, even though he's deaf? Well, I tell ya, ya shouldn't say his name too loud—let me tell you: That H, even if he comes from Czechoslovakia, that man has sure done a swell job of settlin' in to the German psyche.[*]

"Yeah, at least we got order now. Just like yer a citizen and ya got a yellow permit, protected citizen, nothin'll happen to ya ... they're strict about that. Ya gotta admit, it's pretty darn organized. Fantastic! What? At Wittenbergplatz these days? The way they came with their banners and all that music ... not much better under the Kaiser ... Welsch! Hey, a little late there! Movie's already half over. Sit there ... not on my hat! Sit on Regierer's hat—it ain't so new anymore!

"So, Welsch, how goes it? Show me ... I can see ya better in the light. Lookin' good! Did'ja really vote fer the Center Par ... here

---

[*] Hitler actually came from Austria, not from Czechoslovakia, so Wendriner is making a mistake.

come some people from work. Shush! Did'ja really vote fer the Center Party? Meshugge. Oh well, the Center Party put Kareski on the list in his day; that's all just Jewish stuff.* We ... Not so loud! Keep it down! Don't get me in trouble—things are just too tense these days. They're right, after all, expecting us to behave in public. They're absolutely right about that.

"It's starting again. That's Kortner ... see, they're lettin' 'im on the stage, too. I'm just saying, it's ain't so bad at all, right? I think so too. Nice guy. Hey, look. We was jus' talkin' about H. With him, at least ya know he's not stealin' your money. With the Communists, I jus' don't know. Or I know fer sure, what'll happen there. Well, they won't be makin' any moves fer now; they were clobbered. Serves 'em right. That's real politics. Welsch, my dear, the politician should stand on the side of success. Or he ain't no politician. And the businessmen, too. That's real politics. One does the politics, and the other does the real. Damn right.

"Another newsreel? Oh well. Shush! Shuddup about the pictures! Let the people enjoy themselves—it ain't so bad. A really good picture, even ... We saw him close-up the other day; he was standin' there with his under-Führers ... No! Goebbels is outta the picture ... don'cha know that? Hugely popular, even. Maybe because of it. H is payin' close attention. Goebbels wanted ta make an appearance at the Winter Garden ... but they didn't give him no permit.

"Was a little worse today. A little worse. Why? Don't bother askin' at the stock market! The stock market's got a good nose ... jus' don't ask why. Those folks have got a really keen sense of smell—when it's going well, they're real quiet and earning by themselves, and in bad times, they make the others meshugge. And later, they always knew exactly what happened! A pretty picture, jus' look at that! Look, did'ja see that? The way those French soldiers were running

---

* Before the rise of the Nazis, many Berlin Jews voted for the then-liberal DDP (*Deutsche Demokratische Partei*), the so-called State Party. However, after the State Party had merged with the anti-Semitic *Jungdeutsche Orden,* most of Berlin's Jews left the party. Some Jews switched to the Catholic Center Party. George Kareski, an ardent Zionist, captain of industry, and the head of the Jewish community in Berlin from 1928 to 1930, even ran for a seat in the Reichstag on the ticket of the Center Party because he deemed it friendly to the Jews. It was a move widely talked about and criticized within Berlin's Jewish community.

around like crazy? That would never happen with ours! Yeah, even if some are still complainin', I think it's all got its good sides. Jus' think about it yerself ... What for? Whatever for? What does that have to do with the war? What's that Young plan got ta do with the war? Lemme alone! Did we fight the war? We just yelled Hooray. And after that, we didn't have any butter. Oh, shuddup! Since when should people lose a war and pay for it, too? Bad enough, we lost; the others won, so let them pay! Welsch, my dear ... I ... I'm ... Shush!

"I ... Welsch, my dear ... I was expecting certain things in September, too, jus' like you. Oh well, and since I see it ain't like that, I see this system's got its good sides, too. I mean, it's got its historical justification—lemme alone! Ya can't deny it. It's got its ... I mean, the city's got a different look now. And the foreigners are coming again, too, cause they're curious. I gotta say, these folks have got somethin'. I dunno what, but they've got somethin'.

"The end. Well, let's go. Oh, wait, there's the Wessel song. Stand up. What else are ya gonna do—go along with it. By the way ... the English sing their national anthem after the theater, too; so, we Germans just sing a different song ... *March in spirit within our ranks ...*
.

"Pardon me ... It's rainin', huh? Now it's rainin'. Wait, maybe we can get a car. Stand right under there; I'll watch for one. That's no storm troop commander, just' a section leader ... I recognize the emblem. Stand right under there! You should stand under something when it's rainin'. Do we need ta get wet? Let the others get wet. Here comes a car. Here comes the gauleiter.

"Shush! Get in."

---

* The "Horst Wessel Lied" named after an SA Stormtrooper who was killed by Communists, was the official anthem of the Nazi party:

The flag on high! The ranks tightly closed!
The SA march with quiet, steady step.
Comrades shot by the Red Front and reactionaries
March in spirit within our ranks.

Above: Carl von Ossietzky, the editor of Die Weltbühne, in 1934 at Esterwegen, a concentration camp for politcal prisoners. He died in 1938. *Below:* the book burning of 1933 at Opernplatz, today Bebelplatz.

The offices of Die Weltbühne *were at 152 Kantstrasse (**below**) in Charlottenburg. A plaque (**above left**) commemorates its editor Carl von Ossietzky. His predecessor Siegfried Jacobsohn lived nearby in 25 Dernburgstrasse, also in Charlottenburg (**above, right**).*

Röhm

Ignaz Wrobel, Die Weltbühne, April 26, 1932

For a while now, the radical leftist press has printed a stream of accusations, jokes, and digs directed at Captain Röhm, an employee of the Hitler movement. You should never use the ridiculous titles Hitler gives his people, just like you should never accept any of the categories dished out by the Nazis; a lot of Germans succumb to such silly suggestions and approach these things like schoolwork assigned to them by Hitler. We are not in school, and titles, decorations, commendations, and reprimands from this house painter don't mean a thing to us.

So Röhm is gay.

The fuss surrounding him started with publications by the *Münchner Post*, which revealed the fact.

There was also a letter published, in which Röhm wrote about his orientation to a friend—the document could have appeared in any *Psychopathia sexualis*, though the letter wasn't even unpleasant.

I think these attacks on the man miss the point.

Any means are good means against Hitler and his people. Those who treat others so mercilessly are not entitled to mercy—stick it to 'em! In this regard, I wouldn't shy away from the private lives of those involved, either—stick it good! But this goes too far—for all our sakes, it goes too far.

First of all, you should not look for your opponent in bed.

The only thing that might be allowed: pointing out the Nazis' excesses, in which they talk about the "oriental vices" of postwar Germany as if homosexuality, lesbianism and the like were invented by the Russians, who introduced them to the noble, pure, untainted German nation. If a Nazi says something like that, then, and only then, can you say: You have homosexuals in your own movement, who admit to their orientation and are even proud of it—so shut up.

Jokes about Röhm just don't sit right with me. His orientation doesn't disqualify the man at all. He can be entirely decent, as long as he doesn't abuse his position by dragging subordinates to the couch, and there isn't the least scrap of evidence for that. We will fight the disgraceful Paragraph One Hundred Seventy-five wherever we can,* but we cannot then join the choir and ostracize a man just because he's homosexual. Has Röhm committed a public offense? No. Has he pushed himself on young boys? No. Has he intentionally spread venereal diseases? No. These things are subject to public criticism—anything else is his business.

There has been zealous discussion about the important issue of whether or not this employee will stay with Hitler. Are we now the custodians of this private army? Hitler can employ burglars, for all we care.

And when Goebbels screeches or Hitler thunders on about the moral corruption of these modern times, just remind them that there are also homosexuals among the Nazi troops.

Anything else about Röhm's private life means just about as much to us as Hitler's patriotism.

---

* § 175 of the Criminal Code made sex between men illegal. The Nazis sent tens of thousands of gay men to psychiatric clinics or concentration camps, among them a few hundred priests. Between 5,000 and 10,000 were murdered.

Afterward

Kaspar Hauser, Die Weltbühne, September 29, 1925

"Did you learn to swim, when you were alive?" I asked him. We were paddling through endless space, in colorless light; there was no point in moving, because there was no way to determine where we were going. There were no planets to be seen—they were rolling somewhere off in the distance.*

"No," he replied. "I can't swim. I had a hernia. My body had a hernia."

"I didn't learn to swim either," I said. "I always wanted to learn; I started three or four times, but I never succeeded. No, not at swimming. English, neither—it was the same thing. Did you accomplish everything you set out to do? Me neither. And on quiet evenings, when all the fuss of the daily grind had faded and I could catch my breath, then came the hours of reflection and the good intentions. Did that happen to you?"

"Quite often," he said, "Quite often!"

"Yeah, me too," I said. "On evenings like that, you resolved to do so many things. It was clear then that what you were worried about was basically a whole bunch of nonsense that wasn't worth much to anyone, least of all yourself. Those childish invitations! Those completely useless meetings where everything you already knew got harped on for the hundredth time. That endless preaching to the choir! That senseless rushing about in the city, on those ridiculous errands that served no purpose except to be started all over again the next day! What effort everything took, what work, what misery! With the purpose of everything completely forgotten, and everything going off on its own and controlling you! And whenever everything around you grew unusually quiet, so quiet it rang in your ears, then you swore to yourself you'd start a new life."

---

* "Afterward" was the title of another series T. wrote about life after death.

"You even believed it," he said wistfully.

"You definitely believed it!" I said enthusiastically. "You went to bed, full of those beautiful intentions, to really clear out all of the nonsense and really live—just for yourself. And to learn. To learn everything you'd put off, to make up for it all, to overcome all the old laziness and lack of willpower. English and swimming and everything! Then the lawyer calls the next morning, and Aunt Jenny, and the company manager, and you're starting all over again. Then it's done."

"Did you live the life you wanted to live?" he asked, and he didn't wait for a reply. "Of course not. You lived the life that was expected of you—without saying a word, by agreement. You would have been at odds with the whole world if you hadn't—lost friends, been isolated, ended up like some ridiculous hermit. 'He's walling himself in,' they would have said. A reproach. And now it's all over. If you had another chance, how would you do it?" He stopped his swimming motions and looked at me expectantly.

"Exactly the same way," I replied. "Exactly the same."

Above: *The last photo of Kurt Tucholsky, taken in 1935, shortly before his suicide in Hindas, Sweden.* *Right:* *The author at age thirteen, already skeptical of the world.* *Opposite page:* *Tucholsky's grave in Mariefred, Sweden. The inscription reads,* "Alles Vergängliche ist nur ein Gleichnis," *All things transitory are but symbols of the eternal, a line from Goethe's* Faust.

Das Ideal

Ja, das möchste:
Eine **Villa im Grünen**
mit *großer Terrasse*,
vorn die **Ostsee**,
hinten die
Friedrichstraße;
mit schöner Aussicht,
ländlich-mondän,
vom **Badezimmer**
ist die
Zugspitze zu sehn –
aber abends zum **Kino**
hast dus nicht weit.
...
Ja, das möchste!
...

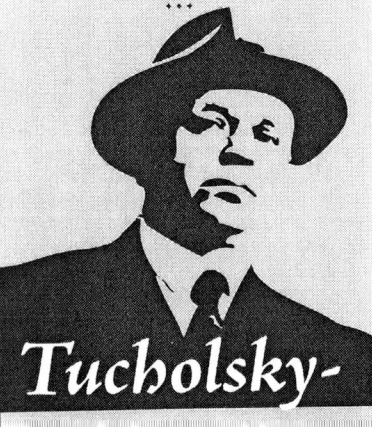

The Ideal

Sure, that's what you want:
A *mansion in the countryside*
with a magnificent porch,
the *Baltic Sea* in front,
Friedrichstrasse
in back;
a wonderful view,
rural chic,
from the *back window*
you can see of the *Alps*
and the *movie theater*
is right around the corner!
... sure you do ...

The Tucholsky
Book Store
in Berlin

**Tucholskystraße 47
10117 Berlin - Mitte**

**tel 01149-30 2757-7663
kurt@buchhandlung-
tucholsky.de
www.buchhandlung-
tucholsky.de
Mon-Sat 10am–7pm**

**Two blocks from S-Bahn
Oranienburger Straße**

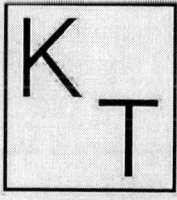

KURT TUCHOLSKY
Literaturmuseum
Schloss Rheinsberg

16831 Rheinsberg
Tel 033 931-39 007
mail@tucholsky-museum.de

Dienstag - Sonntag
April - Oktober   November - März
10:00 - 17:30 Uhr   10:00 - 16:30 Uhr

Mittagspause von 12:30 - 13:00 Uhr

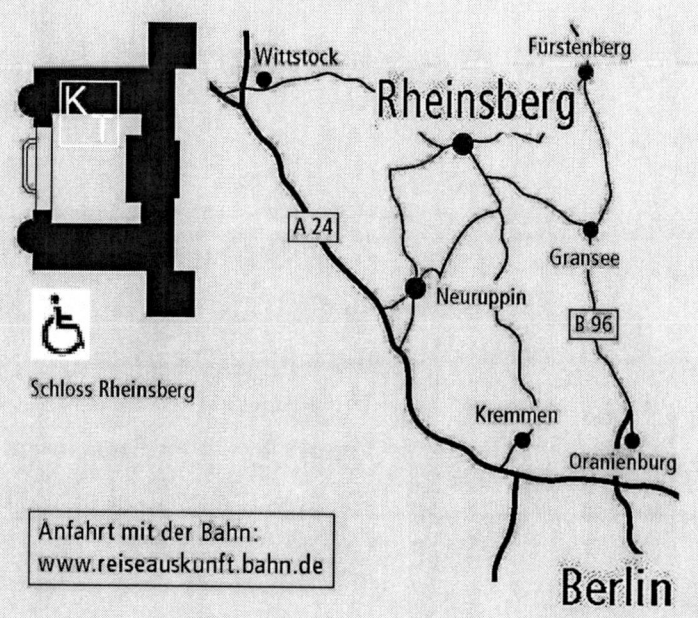

Schloss Rheinsberg

Anfahrt mit der Bahn:
www.reiseauskunft.bahn.de

presents

2010–2017 Program

Subscribe to our newsletter at www.berlinica.com
and get one of the e-books below for free.

New in 2017

Satirical Writings: The Kurt Tucholsky Reader
Translated by Harry Zohn in a New Edition

Kurt Tucholsky

GERMANY? GERMANY!

SATIRICAL WRITINGS
TRANSLATED BY HARRY ZOHN

Preface by Ralph Blumenthal

Softcover, 200 pp., 5 pictures, $14.95
ISBN: 978-1-935902-38-6

**"He was one of the Weimar era's
most acid, incisive satirists."**

Kurt Tucholsky

PRAYER AFTER THE SLAUGHTER

POEMS FROM WORLD WAR I

Bilingual Edition, translated by Peter Appelbaum and James Scott

Softcover, 116 pp., 6 pictures, $12.95, ISBN: 978-1-935902-28-7

"He heaped scorn on the reactionary institutions of the old regime"

Kurt Tucholsky

RHEINSBERG

A STORYBOOK FOR LOVERS

WITH: AMONG CITY WIZARDS
Afterword by Peter Boethig

Hardcover, 96 pp., 35 pictures, $14.95
ISBN: 978-1-935902-25-6

"This book was the blueprint for love for an entire generation"

Andreas Austilat

MARK TWAIN IN BERLIN

NEWLY DISCOVERED STORIES & AN ACCOUNT OF TWAIN'S BERLIN ADVENTURES
Preface by Lewis Lapham

Softcover, 176 pp., 67 pictures, $13.95, ISBN: 978-1-935902-95-9

"This fascinating book is a must-read for any Twain enthusiast"

Cornelia Dömer

MARTIN LUTHER'S TRAVEL GUIDE

500 YEARS OF THE 95 THESES. ON THE TRAIL OF THE REFORMATION IN GERMANY

Softcover, 176 pp., full color
120 pictures and 14 maps, $13.95
ISBN: 978-1-935902-44-7

Sebastian Ringel

LEIPZIG!

ONE THOUSAND YEARS OF GERMAN HISTORY BACH, LUTHER, FAUST: THE CITY OF BOOKS AND MUSIC

Softcover, 224 pp., color, $25.95
ISBN: 978-1-935902-58-1

"Humorous and touching stories from thousand years of Leipzig"

Erik Kirschbaum

BURNING BEETHOVEN

THE ERADICATION OF GERMAN CULTURE IN THE UNITED STATES IN WORLD WAR I

Preface by Herb Stupp

Softcover, 176 pp., 20 pictures,
$14.95, ISBN: 978-1-935902-85-0

"Powerful retelling of a forgotten piece of American history"

Michael Brettin/Peter Kroh

BERLIN 1945

WORLD WAR II:

PHOTOS OF THE AFTERMATH

From the Soviet Army Archives

Preface by Steven Kinzer

Softcover, 218 pp., 177 bw photos
$25.95, ISBN: 978-1-935902-02-7

"Even if you think you've seen it all, Berlin 1945 will surprise you"

Thomas Flemming

BERLIN IN THE COLD WAR–THE BATTLE FOR THE DIVIDED CITY

Softcover, 90 pp., $11.95
51 pictures, 3 maps
ISBN: 978-1-935902-80-5

"The story of a divided city in a nutshell, without missing a beat"

Michael Cramer

THE BERLIN WALL TODAY

REMNANTS, RUINS REMEMBRANCES

Softcover, 100 pp., $15.95
Full color, 150 pictures,
ISBN: 978-1-935902-10-2

"A well-illustrated book"

Erik Kirschbaum

Rocking the Wall

Bruce Springsteen:
The Berlin Concert That Changed the World

Softcover, full color, 168 pp., 45 pict.,
$16.95, ISBN: 978-1-935902-82-9

**"A clear statement of
the power of music"**

Andreas Nachama
Julius Schoeps
Hermann Simon

Jews in Berlin

Preface by Carol Kahn-Strauss

Softcover, 314 pp., $25.95
376 pictures,
ISBN: 978-1-935902-60-7

**". . . a captivating read that pro-
mises a wealth of enjoyment . . ."**

Holly-Jane Rahlens

Wallflower
A Berlin Novel

Softcover, 146 pp., $12.95
ISBN: 978-1-935902-70-6

**". . . an absorbing story of two
people who are trying to figure out
who they are and a fascinating
look at the dawning of a new era
in Germany . . ."**

Berlin for Free
A Guidebook to Music, Movies, Museums
and More for the Frugal Traveler

Originally Published by Verlag an der Spree

Berlinica

Monika Maertens

BERLIN FOR FREE
A GUIDEBOOK TO MOVIES, MUSEUMS, MUSIC, AND MORE FOR THE FRUGAL TRAVELER

Softcover, 104 pp., $11.95
ISBN: 978-1-935902-40-9

"This book is an investment that pays for itself—whoever wants, or has to save, needs it"

Wings of Desire

Angels of Berlin

Lothar Heinke

Lothar Heinke

WINGS OF DESIRE ANGELS OF BERLIN

Softcover, 102 pp., $19.95
Full color, 123 pictures
ISBN: 978-1-935902-18-8

"A book full of anecdotes about the angels throughout the city— and a search for angelic traces"

The Berlin Cookbook
Traditional Recipes and Nourishing Stories
by Rose Marie Donhauser

Berlinica

Rose Marie Donhauser

THE BERLIN COOKBOOK
TRADITIONAL RECIPES AND NOURISHING STORIES

Hardcover, 104 pp., $21.95
61 recipes, 98 color pictures
ISBN: 978-1-935902-51-5

"Beautiful pictures, entertaining texts, and easy to process, fresh ingredients"

Adrienne Haan
BERLIN – MON AMOUR

A TRIBUTE TO 1920s GERMANY IN MUSIC

Music CD, 50 minutes
In English or German
$ 15.95, only on Amazon

"Grace, elegance, power"

The Path To Nuclear Fission
The Story of Lise Meitner and Otto Hahn

A Documentary by Rosemarie Reed
Narrated by Linda Hunt
DVD

Rosemarie Reed
THE PATH TO NUCLEAR FISSION

NARRATED BY LINDA HUNT

Movie DVD, run time 81 min
German / English, subtitled
$19.95, only on Amazon

"... honors the lives of women who were more than significant ..."

THE RED ORCHESTRA
STEFAN ROLOFF

The Red Orchestra was a resistance group that fought against the Third Reich within Germany from 1933 to 1942. The Gestapo labeled them as Communists and traitors for their efforts to put an end to Hitler, a theory that was upheld by Allied Secret Services until recently. Historians now officially recognize their work as that of one of the largest and most efficient Nazi resistance groups. The resistance fighters held a variety of political and religious beliefs. Forty percent of the members were women. Stopping the Third Reich was the common goal. Using a pioneering animation technique, this film tells their story for the first time.

WWW.ROTEKAPELLE-REDORCHESTRA.COM

Stefan Roloff
THE RED ORCHESTRA

A DOCUMENTARY ABOUT THE GERMAN ANTI-NAZI RESISTANCE

Movie DVD, run time 57 min.
German and English, subtitled
$24.95, only on Amazon

". . . danger invaded normalcy . . . landscape threatens to tumble . . ."

Lightning Source UK Ltd.
Milton Keynes UK
UKOW03f1723080517

300758UK00001B/41/P

9 783960 260271